CW01394857

'This is the book that I wish I'd had when starting out as a social entrepreneur. It's rich with ideas and examples, organized around a simple, practical model. It'll be invaluable to anyone who aspires to get stuck in and really make a difference.'

Tom Ravenscroft, Founder & CEO, Skills Builder Partnership

'A much-needed practical guide to help anyone turn a good idea into a life-changing social enterprise!'

Natasha Porter OBE, Founder & CEO, Unlocked Graduates

'Required reading for all those willing to dedicate their life's work to making a difference.'

Vikas Pota, Founder & CEO, T4 Education

'Drawing on his experience as a charity founder, Jo articulates a formula for changing the world that has such resonance with my own experience I found myself nodding along as I was reading. I only wish this practical step-by-step guide on how to ignite the spark of an idea had existed when I started out. A must-read.'

Dr Nicola Sharp-Jeffs, Founder, Surviving Economic Abuse

'A well-timed book; the blueprint to making your idea a reality and changing the world. Take your dream, read this, and let it fly.'

Jo Youle OBE, CEO, Missing People

'With its clear, practical and pragmatic steps, this guide is invaluable for anyone who wants to change the world! At times, ruthlessly honest (and demanding the same from its reader), yet consistently inspiring and thought-provoking. Jo does not shy away from uncomfortable truths.'

Steve Cutts, Chair, UNFPA Oversight Advisory Committee; Former United Nations and Commonwealth Assistant Secretary-General

HOW TO CHANGE THE WORLD

Jo Owen

How social entrepreneurs
can go from initial ideas
to global impact

BLOOMSBURY

BLOOMSBURY BUSINESS
Bloomsbury Publishing Plc
50 Bedford Square, London, WC1B 3DP, UK
Bloomsbury Publishing Ireland Limited,
29 Earlsfort Terrace, Dublin 2, D02 AY28, Ireland

BLOOMSBURY, BLOOMSBURY BUSINESS and the Diana logo are trademarks of
Bloomsbury Publishing Plc

First published in Great Britain 2025

Copyright © Jo Owen, 2025

Jo Owen has asserted his right under the Copyright, Designs and Patents Act, 1988, to be
identified as Author of this work

All rights reserved. No part of this publication may be: i) reproduced or transmitted in
any form, electronic or mechanical, including photocopying, recording or by means of any
information storage or retrieval system without prior permission in writing from the publishers;
or ii) used or reproduced in any way for the training, development or operation of artificial
intelligence (AI) technologies, including generative AI technologies. The rights holders
expressly reserve this publication from the text and data mining exception as per Article 4(3) of
the Digital Single Market Directive (EU) 2019/790

Bloomsbury Publishing Plc does not have any control over, or responsibility for, any third-
party websites referred to or in this book. All internet addresses given in this book were
correct at the time of going to press. The author and publisher regret any inconvenience
caused if addresses have changed or sites have ceased to exist, but can accept no
responsibility for any such changes

A catalogue record for this book is available from the British Library

Library of Congress Cataloging-in-Publication data has been applied for

ISBN: 978-1-3994-2449-3; eBook: 978-1-3994-2450-9

2 4 6 8 10 9 7 5 3 1

Typeset by Deanta Global Publishing Services, Chennai, India
Printed and bound in Great Britain by Clays Ltd, Elcograf S.p.A.

MIX
Paper | Supporting
responsible forestry
FSC
www.fsc.org   FSC® C018072

To find out more about our authors and books visit www.bloomsbury.com
and sign up for our newsletters

For product safety related questions contact productsafety@bloomsbury.com

CONTENTS

INTRODUCTION

Everyone is always changing the world. What we do and how we do it affects our family, friends and colleagues for better or for worse. But some people change the world more than others. Some succeed because they are geniuses, some because they are lucky and some because they are rich and powerful. But you do not need to be a genius, lucky, rich or powerful to have a profound effect on our world. All you need is an idea, and to make it happen.

Just as everyone has a book in them, so everyone has an idea in them which can change the world. Your idea can come from anywhere: from reading an article, talking to colleagues, stumbling across a good idea which can be developed. It is often tempting to say 'someone should do something about that'. But why shouldn't that 'someone' be you?

This book shows how people like you have taken an idea and turned it into something which is changing the world. Your idea does not need to remain a pipe dream, it can become reality. This book shows how you can perform the miracle of creating something great out of nothing.

The simplest way to read it is as a manual on how you can change the world. Although every journey to success is different, there are six consistent principles: Idea, Impact, People, Partnerships, Money and a Machine. This deceptively simple formula is called IPM squared and will help you plot your journey from idea to impact at scale.

The book is organized around the IPM squared formula:

- Idea: Find the spark of an idea to change the world
- Impact: Adapt your idea so it has impact and is scalable, replicable and sustainable

- People: Create and sustain the winning team
- Partnerships: Build the coalitions which will take your idea to scale
- Money: Find it, manage it and make the most of it
- Machine: Build the machine to run your idea effectively.

The final section of the book takes you from a worm's-eye to bird's-eye view of the world. The worm's-eye view challenges many of the beliefs about development that come from having a bird's-eye view of the world. The reality on the ground is very different from the reality seen from the air. The book shows that there are different ways to think about:

- Charitable organizations and non-governmental organizations (NGOs)
- Philanthropy
- Development aid
- Monitoring and evaluation (M&E).

The bird's-eye view of these issues leads to fairly sterile debates among the usual suspects in the usual places, such as Davos and UNGA (the UN General Assembly). In contrast, the worm's-eye view shows how to use today's charitable and development efforts far better. It shows how a vast waste of time, money and effort can be avoided. The best ideas achieve real development, not dependency. Average ideas often do more harm than good.

HOW EVERYONE CHANGES THE WORLD ALL THE TIME

It was rush hour and my feet were on autopilot as they walked me to the office. As I passed a fancy office block, I noticed the doorman. He was very smartly dressed, with brown and white two-tone shoes. 'Natty shoes, love them!' I exclaimed as I passed

---

him. A big broad smile broke out over his face and he suddenly seemed to grow two inches taller.

On the return rush hour he spotted me in the crowd and shouted, 'How was your day, sir?' It had, in fact been very good, not least because I had felt very good about his reaction earlier in the day. And because I was feeling good during the day, people around me were responding positively. It was a virtuous circle: they felt good, which made me feel good, which made them feel good.

'Excellent, how was yours?' I replied.

The doorman beamed again: 'One of the best, thank you very much!'

Clearly, he was having a good day, which made everyone else have a good day. I like to think that my 'natty shoes' comment at the start of the day had started his day well.

We all experience moments when strangers make us feel better about the world; we also have moments when the behaviour of strangers makes us discover our inner axe-wielding maniac. Every day, in your smallest interactions with the world, you make the world better or worse. You cannot avoid changing the world.

HOW THIS BOOK CAME ABOUT

This book is the product of working for over 20 years with charities and development organizations across the world. In that time, I have been fortunate to become a founder, co-founder or chair of eight great NGOs. They have achieved a collective turnover in excess of $100 million. Some of these organizations have been great successes: Teach First is now the largest graduate recruiter in the UK; STIR is helping over 6 million children get great education with great teachers. Others have been more modestly successful and a couple have not (yet) fulfilled their promise. All of them have been a very rich source of learning about what does – and does not – work. Much of that learning is reflected in this book.

One driver of this book has been frustration and anger. There is far too much waste of people's time and money:

- Many charities remediate failed government policies, but charity should never be a substitute for good government. This is as true of developed countries as it is of developing countries.
- Too much aid increases dependency and props up weak, incompetent or corrupt governments.
- Too many NGO and charity boards are more focused on scaling their organization than on scaling their mission. They chase the money and dance to the tune of their funders. Like latter-day imperialists, their real goal is to plant as many of their flags on the world map as possible.
- Too much philanthropic and aid funding deals with symptoms, not causes, of problems. In the short term, they can show results but in the long term, nothing changes. They measure and evaluate the wrong things, the wrong way over the wrong time horizon.
- Too many charities offer piecemeal solutions to symptoms of problems, not the cause of the problem. System level change is often required and rarely achieved.

The good news is that there are bright spots of great organizations achieving great things. The focus of this book is on the bright spots who show what is possible. Being angry and frustrated achieves nothing, nor does a polemic against what is happening today. The worm's-eye view of what actually works, and how it works, gives policy makers and funders the insight to increase the effectiveness of what they do massively. Out of anger comes hope.

Although the book is focused on the not-for-profit sector, the reality is that for-profit firms can also be a huge force for good. Most of the technology we take for granted today has been largely developed by private sector firms: life without computing, telecoms, artificial intelligence (AI) and pharmaceuticals would be uncomfortable for us. For-profit can be a highly effective way of changing the world, not least because it is far easier to scale and to manage for-profit firms. The reality is that managing in the not-for-profit world is far harder than managing in the for-profit world. This book will show you why this is the case and what you can do about it.

ABOUT THE BOOK

This book is based on extensive research; over 50 cases are used here. The research has included over 100 formal interviews and countless informal discussions over the past 20 years. In addition, I have drawn on the extensive research literature which already exists. Some of the literature is high-level policy, some of it is focused on specific case examples. Throughout, I reference the research as appropriate so that you can follow up and form your own opinions.

I use the terms NGO and charity somewhat interchangeably throughout the book. Clearly, not all NGOs are charities (UNICEF, for instance). Where an NGO is clearly not a charity, I use the term NGO. Charities operate under specific legal and regulatory requirements which not all NGOs face: where this is the case, I use the term charity.

As ever, practice is a humbling antidote to theory. This is where I am hugely grateful to all the staff, board members and CEOs of the various organizations I have chaired or helped to found. I have learned, and continue to learn, a huge amount from them. I am also deeply grateful to everyone who has helped make the book happen: the countless people who have given me their time, insight and advice: Ian Hallsworth and Allie Collins, and the wonderful team at Bloomsbury who had the courage and vision to take on this idea, and to my wife Hiromi, who once again became a book widow while I wrote the book.

Despite all this help, mistakes and controversies are more or less inevitable in such a large and complex topic: they are all my responsibility.

HOW YOU CAN CHANGE THE WORLD

The purpose of this book is to show you how you can find your great idea and turn it into reality. The good news is that you do not need personal brilliance, wealth or networks to start out. You do not even need the perfect idea or solution, because every great idea starts as a half-formed idea which evolves to greatness.

The day-to-day reality of starting and scaling an organization is far messier than the simple narratives you will find in research papers. It is also much more fun and, occasionally, frustrating and frightening. So this book will not present you with a sanitized picture of how to change the world. Inevitably, your noble goal is likely to be challenged by frauds, thefts, crime, legal cases, staff disasters, near-death experiences as you run out of cash and deal with chaotic politics, intransigent and corrupt bureaucrats, exasperating funders. These are the sort of challenges which make changing the world such a rich and rewarding way to live. By exploring this dark side of success, I hope you will either avoid making the same mistakes or you will be able to remedy them when you encounter them. Knowing that these disasters are normal, and not all your fault, is in itself reassuring.

There are plenty of reasons why you might not want to take on the challenge: you have other battles to fight, you have a career to manage and a family to feed. And there is the nagging fear that maybe your idea is not so simple and it may not succeed. After all, it takes courage to pursue your dream.

HOW TO CHANGE THE WORLD AT WORK

Whenever I visit a school, I have to find a way to engage kids of all ages. After many failures, I stumbled across a sure-fire way of starting a big conversation. I ask the class: 'Have you ever been taught by an unhappy teacher?'

Immediately, a forest of small arms shoots up. Everyone is keen to tell me just how awful it is to be taught by an unhappy teacher, and how obvious it is that teacher is unhappy. Then I ask them to talk about their experience of a happy teacher. Enthusiasm levels rise immediately. Normally, the happy teacher is the one where the children are most engaged, learn the most and they find it is their favourite subject and favourite teacher.

As with the classroom, so too with the office. We all know what it is like to have a miserable boss or colleague. Their little cloud of gloom can spread like a major depression across the whole office. A positive boss is like a breath of fresh air that spreads energy wherever they go.

Choosing how we feel and how we are has a huge impact on our colleagues, friends and family. You are changing the world every moment of the day, simply by the way you are, so choose well.

What you do, what you say and how you behave means that you are changing the world every moment of every day. You cannot tell what the ultimate effect of your actions may be. Like the tale of the flapping of the butterfly's wings in the Amazon which eventually leads to a failure of the monsoon in India, chaos theory indicates that the smallest action can have huge unintended impacts.

But some people have much greater and much more intentional impacts on the world than others. These people are not freaks of nature who become billionaires, Nobel Prize-winning scientists or world leaders. They are (relatively) ordinary people who achieve extraordinary things: they are people like you.

This book is about how you can come up with an idea to change the world and make it happen.

1

Idea

Ignite the spark to change the world

This chapter will show you how to:

- *Come up with an idea to change the world*
- *Know if your idea is workable*
- *Pivot to success.*

This chapter shows that you do not need to be a genius to come up with a world-changing idea. It also shows how you can develop your idea and strategy without recourse to consultants. Here, you will discover why changing the world depends on outsiders and innovators challenging the status quo. You do not need to be an insider or expert. Many of the large-legacy NGOs struggle to challenge and change the world as it is. Finally, changing the world and making a profit can walk hand in hand: do not assume that the profit motive is morally inferior.

COME UP WITH AN IDEA TO CHANGE THE WORLD
The world is changed by great ideas and there is no such thing as a great idea which never happened. Your idea can only be great if it

turns into reality. These great ideas come in endless forms. In retrospect, each idea is obvious:

- Google: paid search
- Social networks (Instagram, YouTube, TikTok) build your network and get the dopamine hit from 'likes'
- Einstein: $e = mc^2$
- Grameen Bank: microfinance to lift the poorest out of poverty.

All of these ideas have changed the world for better or for worse. Although they look obvious now, they were not obvious at the time. Before Google came along, many smart people had thrown billions of dollars at varying attempts to become the search engine of choice: Microsoft made various attempts, as did Excite, Lycos, Infoseek and many others. They have all become no more than footnotes in history.

Finding the spark which will set the world alight
The chances are that you have already had that great idea. It may have come in a conversation with friends; it might have come when you saw something in the news and got annoyed because there seemed to be a simple solution to the news story; it may be you have seen a better way of doing things in your area of work.

The chance for inspiration can come from anywhere, anytime. For instance, Mark Evans was reading a copy of *The Times* online when he noticed a letter from the Saudi Arabian ambassador. The letter pointed out that England had taken a 600-year journey to democracy and perhaps people should be a little bit more patient with Saudi Arabia's development path. Most people would either not read the letter or shrug their shoulders and move on to the sports, business or other pages.

Mark thought that the ambassador had a point and so he wrote a short note to the ambassador saying that it would be a good idea if there could be more mutual understanding, especially among the next generation. To his surprise, the ambassador invited Mark to tea.

That started a series of conversations which led to the creation of the magnificently named University of the Desert.* This is a virtual university which brings young people from different cultures together in the desert. They not only explore and understand the desert, they explore and understand each other's cultures.

STARTING TEACH FIRST

Teach First is now the largest graduate recruiter in the UK. It recruits great graduates to teach in some of the most disadvantaged areas in the UK. At the time, this was a revolutionary idea. Graduates from the top universities did not see teaching as an attractive career proposition. In the areas which Teach First targeted, precisely zero teachers had graduated from Oxford or Cambridge Universities. So how does anyone with no experience of education come up with an idea like Teach First?

The idea came from listening to the radio. KFOG-FM interrupted its normal mix of classic rock to do a short interview with a graduate who was teaching in the inner city in San Francisco. Hooked, I rang the station to get the name of the project, which was called Teach for America. I then called Teach for America and asked to speak with the CEO, Wendy Kopp. Having a fruity British accent, I was put straight through. I asked her to bring Teach for America to the UK. She said she was too busy, but I might like to talk to some people at McKinsey & Company who were doing some research for the Prince of Wales (now King Charles) about education in London. I called McKinsey and was put through to a researcher called Brett Wigdortz. We then sat down and agreed to develop a modified version of Teach for America in England.

Hearing that initial interview, my first inclination was to switch stations. My second instinct was to file the interview

---

*The University of the Desert now exists as a project within Outward Bound Oman. https://outwardboundoman.com/desert-learning-centre/

in the 'interesting but forget' mental file, but the reality is that opportunities are being thrown at us all the time. You do not have to come up with a brilliant idea that no one has ever thought of before.

You do not even need to be an expert in the area. All the ideas are out there already, waiting to be taken up and adapted by anyone.

Look at the news, read the papers, listen to the radio today: somewhere you will find the germ of an idea which can change the world.

Like many great ideas, both the University of the Desert and Teach First emerged from drinking plenty of tea and talking at length about an idea. Tea, not money or genius, is the fuel of great ideas. It is rare for ideas to emerge fully formed and perfect from day one. In practice, most new ideas do not dazzle like the bright midday sun. The great idea may be there, waiting to emerge slowly from the darkness. Like a solitary, flickering candle, they must be nurtured and protected. This was the case for one of the most famous change-the-world ideas of all: Grameen Bank, which started up the idea of microfinancing. Microfinancing has helped lift millions of people out of poverty not by giving them aid, but by giving them loans. The loans may be as small as a few dollars. That's enough to buy some corn or chickens, or to start a small urban business which can transform the fortunes of a family.

Grameen achieves a staggering 97 per cent recovery rate on the loans it makes to the poorest in society.* It does this not through the traditional methods of informal lenders, which often involve coercion. Grameen developed the idea of 'social capital'. Instead of lending to one person at a time, they would lend to groups of five to ten people, typically women. This is transformative. Groups of borrowers work

---

*Grameen Annual Report, 2022, pp. 17–18.

together: peer group pressure and support replaces the adversarial relationship between borrower and lender. These small groups, based on mutual trust and dependency, solve problems together, innovate and make the loans work effectively.

Grameen's model has been widely copied to help some of the poorest communities around the world. It is now seen as a fairly standard tool for economic development. As ever, what is obvious after the event was seen to be mad before it. Banks would never lend to such poor people: they have no collateral, they are seen to be very poor credit risks and the cost of serving them is prohibitive for such small sums. The only source of credit they had were loan sharks, who would drive them into debt bondage. The poor were one bad harvest away from the twin disasters of starvation and debt bondage. To see how radical Grameen is compared to traditional finance or charity, it is worth looking at its main beliefs:

- Poverty is not the fault of the poor: it is caused by the institutions and policies which surround the poor;
- Charity does not solve poverty, it perpetuates poverty by creating dependency;
- Trust the poor: they are as willing and as able as the rich to repay loans;
- Bank loans should go to those who need it the most, not to those who have the most;
- Lending to women is more productive than lending to men.

These beliefs were an all-out assault on some of the most dearly-held beliefs of charities and banks.

The idea for Grameen emerged slowly. Like many great ideas, it started as a response to a crisis. Bangladesh was emerging from a major famine which had devastated the economy in 1974. Professor of Economics Dr Muhammad Yunus was well aware of the poverty which surrounded his university campus. In 1976, he visited Jobra, a nearby village, and he personally loaned a grand total of $27 to 42 villagers to help them rebuild their lives. Yunus was not clear whether it would work or whether he would ever see his money again. In his words:

> *'I gave money from my pocket. I did not know that it would create an emotional counter response from the people who got the money. They thought it was nothing less than a miracle. I started giving loans to these poor people in Jobra and was pleasantly surprised to see that it was working perfectly."*

That $27 was the small spark which set the world alight with a revolutionary way of addressing poverty. As we shall see later in this book, the idea had to be developed and nurtured carefully for years before it became scalable. It was seven years before Grameen Bank was formally established. It takes time for great ideas to mature and seven years is typical. Once the model for Grameen Bank was firmly established, it grew phenomenally. The initial $27 loan blossomed into cumulative $38 billion of loans to over 10 million members by 2024[†] and the model has been widely copied elsewhere. The bank is 94 per cent owned by its borrowers and 6 per cent owned by the Government of Bangladesh. In 2006, Professor Yunus won the Nobel Prize for Peace. The biggest ideas start with the smallest spark.

The three cases which illustrate the initial spark of an idea at first appear to be wildly different:

- University of the Desert in Oman
- Teach First for top graduates to teach in England
- Microfinance for the very poor, in Bangladesh.

But behind the differences are some simple lessons to be learned:

[*]Social Capital and Microfinance: The Case of Grameen Bank, Bangladesh. Article – October 2013 DOI: 10.5742/MEJB.2013.84311 Dewan Mahboob Hossain, University of Dhaka.
[†]https://grameenbank.org.bd/about/introduction. Outstanding loans are over $1.5 billion in 2024; 98 per cent of borrower members are female.

- Your idea to change the world can come from anywhere: listening to the radio, reading the news, fixing a problem on your doorstep.
- Great ideas do not need a great amount of money to start with. They need a great amount of imagination, which often comes from talking about your idea with other people.
- Great ideas often take time to succeed. As with all plans, they do not survive first contact with reality. Truly great ideas change and adapt.
- Great ideas need passionate advocates who will nurture the idea in the face of hostility and indifference.
- Outsiders are often the best revolutionaries: they do not understand that what they are doing is meant to be impossible. Yunus was a professor, not a banker; Mark Evans had no idea about universities and Teach First was founded by people with no experience of education.

These lessons will be explored later in the book. The salient point is that neither money nor experience are obstacles to success. In each case, there were myriad obstacles and objections to be overcome. The hallmark of a great idea is that each time it encounters an objection, it finds a solution which strengthens the idea.

The biggest obstacle to your idea is not external, it is in your head. Your internal fears and demons will be amplified by well-meaning friends and experts who unhelpfully point out all the risks and problems you need to overcome. This sort of help is like a cancer which will slowly kill your idea. Fortunately, you may also talk to people who see solutions where other people see problems. These people self-select themselves onto your team as employees, volunteers and advisors. Cherish them because they are your future.

HOW DO YOU KNOW IF YOUR IDEA IS A WINNER?

Generals like to say that most battles are won and lost before the first shot is fired, although they do not say that to troops who are about to go into battle. The same is true of most charities and

NGOs: their success or failure is largely determined before they even start. Success is determined by the quality of the idea and the quality of the people. If you have a great idea and great people, you are on your way to success. If your idea is the wrong idea, then it is finished before it starts. That means you need to get the idea right from the outset.

The challenge is that you never know if your idea is a winner until it has either won or lost. You need some way of finding out whether you should commit a large part of your life to chasing a dream: will it turn into reality or turn out to be fantasy? You do not need to have all the right answers, but you do need to have the right questions. As you explore and develop your idea, you should ask yourself four questions. These are the four main questions which funders, philanthropists and governments should ask about all charities and NGOs:

- What is the impact?
- Is your idea scalable, replicable and sustainable?
- Is your idea different and/or better than existing programmes?
- Does it attract great people?

These questions are easy to ask and hard to answer. You will not have the answers yourself. The only way you can find some answers is by talking to people: friends and colleagues, potential supporters, experts and potential beneficiaries of your idea.

Here is what to look for in the big four questions:

What is the impact?
You can think of impact at three levels:

- Symptom relief: dealing with immediate distress and dependency
- Symptom cures: achieving short-term impact but not addressing underlying problems
- System change: dealing with the root causes of the problem.

Symptom relief ranges from disaster relief to palliative care in hospices. These are important and worthy, even if they do not solve the cause of the problem. In some cases, relief work is accused of increasing dependency and increasing the original problem. The work of Sea-Watch 3* and other ships in saving migrants in the Mediterranean incurred the wrath of the Italian government, who claimed that such rescue work was really doing the work of the people smugglers. The implication was that they were making the problem worse by encouraging people smuggling, not better by saving migrants from drowning.

There is a need for organizations to deliver symptom relief. Communities which suffer from natural disasters, war and famine need help to recover. Short-term survival is the first step to long-term recovery. The focus of this book is not on short-term survival, but on ideas which can help people and communities transform sustainably over the long term.

Symptom relief can be dangerous. A classic example is to give money to a homeless person begging on the street. You need a heart of stone to ignore their desperation. John (now Lord) Bird had first-hand experience of this desperation. First made homeless at the age of five, he became an orphan and drifted into crime and prison. He decided to address the challenge of homelessness by starting the *Big Issue* in 1991 which has now been copied around the world. The *Big Issue* is a professionally produced magazine which the homeless can sell on the street to earn a living. His experience showed that the homeless do not need a handout. Giving them money is like cementing their feet to the pavement: it simply buys them their next fix and perpetuates their misery. In his words: 'by reinforcing the beggar's pitiable condition, a donation is really an act of cruelty

---

*Colleen Berry: Italy's Salvini furious as 47 migrants land despite his ban. *Washington Post*, 20 May 2019. This was typical of the widespread coverage at the time, which was a topic of great controversy.

rather than kindness." Random acts of kindness can do more harm than good.

Symptom cures are much loved of funders. They see a problem such as low levels of literacy in a community and they fund an organization to deliver a literacy programme to fix the problem. They can then measure the impact of different programmes to see which programme leads to the most improvement at the best cost. At first glimpse, this is the sweet spot for any intervention. It is targeted, measurable and manageable. You can run RCTs (Randomized Control Trials) to test the effectiveness of different approaches. So what's not to like about such an approach?

The problem with symptom cures is that they rarely address underlying problems, which means that the 'cure' is not sustainable.

DEALING WITH SYMPTOMS OR CAUSES?

Literacy is the gateway to learning. If you are illiterate, you will struggle to learn anything. In many marginal communities, girls' literacy levels are very low. So what can you do about it?

To address this challenge, the UK government launched a 12-year initiative: the Girl's Education Challenge.[†] The obvious solution would be to introduce some literacy programmes but that would not work unless the communities accepted the programme and the system and committed to it for the long term. A short-term fix would have a short-term impact and be forgotten.

As part of this programme, I found myself in the middle of the African bush holding a community conversation with about 300 people in Lokichar[‡], a Turkana village. The discussion was about whether girls should receive a proper education. There were

---

'John Bird, *Daily Mail*, 5 November 2014. https://www.dailymail.co.uk/news/article-2821189 /Giving-money-beggars-isn-t-kindness-Ed-s-cruelty-know-used-one-says-founder-Big-Issue -JOHN-BIRD.html
[†]https://girlseducationchallenge.org/about/
[‡]The author is now an Elder of Lokichar.

arguments that educating girls would lead to poverty: the more a girl is educated, the more likely she is to leave the community to work elsewhere and her family will lose a vital dowry payment. Then there was discussion about what it would take to get girls educated. They would need not just a school, they would need latrines. Without latrines, girls do not want to go to school. And they need uniforms, underwear and female sanitary protection. And the community would need to start protecting them from sexual assault on the way to and from school. No one even bothered to discuss what sort of literacy programme might be required, so many other factors needed to be put in place first.

In addition to the villagers' concerns, we had to work out how to find teachers who were not just qualified, but also had the intrinsic motivation to teach in what amounted to a hardship posting. They in turn had to be supported by officials at all levels who understood the programme and backed the teachers. The programme would be as strong as its weakest link.

Even this systemic solution is not sustainable unless it can be funded sustainably. The UK government programme could pump prime the solution, but cannot sustain it. Educating one cohort of girls and leaving the next cohort to fend for themselves is close to immoral.

Many organizations deliver wonderful literacy programmes but they can only flourish in the right context. You have to look beyond the symptom of the problem (poor literacy) to the causes. This normally leads you to work on changing the whole system, not just one part of it.

System change looks beyond the immediate problem and seeks solutions to the underlying cause. Grameen Bank explicitly recognizes this. It does not simply give loans to the poorest in society. The bank wraps the loan in a support package which will enable the recipients to make the most of their loan. The bedrock of their lending programme is 'solidarity lending' where loans are made to groups of five or more individuals. Although each individual is responsible for their loan, the group approach builds peer support and pressure. Many borrowers are illiterate and are not required to sign any loan documentation. Instead, they have to recite the 16 'decisions' or principles of Grameen Bank,* which include:

- We shall grow vegetables all the year round. We shall eat plenty of them and sell the surplus.
- During the planting seasons, we shall plant as many seedlings as possible.
- We shall plan to keep our families small. We shall minimize our expenditures. We shall look after our health.
- We shall educate our children and ensure that they can earn to pay for their education.
- We shall always keep our children and the environment clean.
- We shall build and use pit-latrines.

Grameen's relationship with its borrowers is based on trust, not on legal forms. Grameen does not focus simply on money, it focuses on helping clients build a healthy and (relatively) wealthy lifestyle.

If your idea is about system change, you have started the journey to changing the world but system change comes with a whole host of challenges:

- It is very difficult to achieve
- Success takes a long time
- Funders will be reluctant to support you: many prefer the instant gratification of symptom cures

*"Guidelines for establishing and operating Grameen-style Microcredit programs", M. Nurul Alam and Dr Mike Getubig. Grameen Trust 2010.

- The idea you start with will more or less certainly not be the one which succeeds: you will have to keep on learning and adapting.

But you should remember that if changing the world was so easy, someone would have done so already. The fact that your idea is difficult shows that you are taking on a genuinely worthwhile challenge.

This book is about exploring how you can change systems to change the world.

Is your idea scalable, replicable and sustainable?
If you want to change the world, your idea has to be scalable, replicable and sustainable:

- Scalable: ideas often work at small scale because they are fuelled by the passion of the founders and they often have relatively high cost per intervention. But to change the world, you need scale without relying on passion and without high cost.
- Replicable: your idea has to work across multiple contexts and conditions. That means you have to find the magic sauce behind your idea which makes a difference around the world, not just in one location.
- Sustainable: your idea has to be sustainable over time. It has to be economically sustainable at scale: how will it be funded? And it needs to be operationally sustainable: you need a stable machine to deliver results.

The three challenges of scaling, replicating and sustaining are the fundamental challenges for any idea which changes the world. Here's what the three challenges mean in practice:

The scaling challenge. Anyone who works in the voluntary sector will soon find themselves meeting extraordinary people who achieve extraordinary things, often with little money but huge enthusiasm and effort. These are the people who dedicate themselves to addressing the toughest challenges of society: the environment, climate change, homelessness, poverty, substance abuse, crime and re-offending, mental illness and access to justice to name but a few causes. Without these efforts, all these problems would be far worse. But even with the efforts of so many talented and committed people, these challenges remain as intractable as ever.

How can so many great people doing great things appear to have no effect on the system as a whole? The problem in many cases is one of scalability. The success of these great ideas is fuelled by the passion and inspiration of the founder of the charity. Unfortunately, you cannot scale passion and inspiration.

LET A THOUSAND FLOWERS WILT

Many prisoners are highly entrepreneurial: if you are a drug dealer you have to learn how to manage supply chains, manage distribution, meet demand, segment the market, price competitively and collect debts. You also need a keen sense of risk management given that mistakes can lead to arrest, imprisonment, assault, injury or death. We found that many prisoners could re-apply their skills to brilliant ideas from the normal (plumbers, gardeners and fitness coaches) to the abnormal (Buddy Holly tribute act, split-screen combi van spare parts, wig makers and roti cooks). These are people who would do very badly in a traditional organization, taking orders from a boss they despise, but they succeeded brilliantly as entrepreneurs.

We built a programme to help these entrepreneurial prisoners build legitimate businesses on release from prison. Of our first 400 prisoners, fewer than ten re-offended: normally, 66 per cent of prisoners are expected to re-offend within two years. This was a staggering success. We were so confident of our idea that we were prepared to work on a no-win no-fee basis: the government would only pay us if our clients did not re-offend.

The Prisons Minister duly kicked us out. There were several reasons for this. Part of the problem was that the Ministry of Justice was entirely dysfunctional. It was focused on putting people in prison, not on keeping them out, and the civil servants could not understand that self-employment is different from employment. But the real problem was scale.

The Prisons Minister gave his verdict: 'There are a thousand wonderful charities out there, all doing their bit for rehabilitation. But you cannot base a national policy on one thousand conflicting and confusing initiatives. That is the road to chaos. Come back and show me you can deliver this at national scale and perhaps we can have another conversation.'

The Prisons Minister may have been searching for an excuse to do nothing, but he had found a good excuse. National problems require national solutions. It also requires an integrated solution: some offenders may be able to start businesses, but others need help with housing, addiction, relationships, mental health, literacy and numeracy and basic skills. All the work of the many rehabilitation charities did not add up to a coherent, scalable and sustainable solution to the problem of re-offending. Re-offending might be far worse without their efforts, but despite all their efforts, re-offending remains a huge problem. In the UK, it will only get worse: prison overcrowding means that offenders are being released early, without rehabilitation or support.

By definition, if you want to change the world, you have to be bold and think big. This is not about bragging and boasting, it is about clearly understanding what it will take to make the change you want to make. Policy makers need a few big ideas, not thousands of small ideas. They are more likely to listen to you if you have an idea which meets the scale of their challenge.

You do not need to be bold or courageous to think big. You just need to be realistic about what it will take to bring your idea to fruition. This is your road to credibility. Pretending that you can change the world in a morning with just two dollars is not credible. Advertising posters pretending that cancer or hunger or any other worthy cause can be fixed with a donation of $5 a month lack credibility or integrity. You gain respect through brutal honesty. Be clear with yourself and your partners about what it will take to succeed.

The surprise is that it is easier to think big than to think small. Big ideas attract attention from big players, funders and partners. They also attract more support and more opposition. At least your idea will not die of indifference. And even the opposition is helpful: it tells you who and what obstacles to success lie in store for you. The more engagement you get, the more you can refine and improve your idea.

THINKING BIG BEATS THINKING SMALL

For various unlikely reasons, I decided to start a bank. I did the calculations and realized that starting the bank would require over $1 billion of capital. I checked my bank account and found that I was more than $1 billion short of the required funding. So I started to build a business case by talking to various experts. The $1 billion figure slowly became more robust and credible.

Eventually, I found myself talking to the CEO of a bank who was interested in incubating this new idea: it would let them compete in the small- to medium-size business market where they had a feeble presence. I knew this was going to be the big discussion because we did not sit at his conference table: we were sitting on comfy sofas in his vast office. That is where all serious discussions happen.

Eventually, he asked how much the idea would cost. 'About a billion,' I replied as casually as I could, remembering to say 'billion' not 'million'. He did not bat an eyelid. 'Good,' he said, 'if you had asked for any less, you would not have been credible.'

In that one conversation I made several discoveries:

- It is easier to ask for 1,000 million dollars from a bank than it is to ask for 1,000 dollars.
- If you have a big idea, you will meet the right people: you will meet the CEO of the bank who has decision making power, not a junior relationship manager who has no discretionary power.
- People are more excited by big ideas than small ideas: you will get more support and more opposition but at least you will not get indifference.
- Thinking big is a consequence of thinking clearly about your idea. It is not about being bold, it is about being realistic, which in turn enhances your credibility.

The replication challenge is related, but different, to the scaling challenge. An obvious way to achieve scale is to replicate your programme many times. For instance, if you have set up and run a successful school, you cannot scale that one school to cover the entire country. Instead, you could try to replicate the school by setting up (or taking over) lots of other schools around the country. Many have tried to replicate success at one school into other schools, but few have succeeded. Replicating school success is hard for two reasons:

- Conditions vary between schools and areas. What works in a leafy lane suburb may not translate into an economically deprived inner-city estate.
- Success is often down to the inspiration and charisma of the head teacher and key members of the teaching staff. There is no known formula for replicating inspiration and medical science has not invented a charisma transplant service, yet.

Often the winning formula only works because of the energy and passion of the founder who has developed a site specific solution. Even large organizations find it hard to replicate success: Grameen

Bank has been very successful in Bangladesh but has struggled to replicate its success in other countries. Essentially, it is having to relearn and adapt its success formula into each country.

Replication is possible, as Teach for All has shown. Teach for All was founded in 2007 by Teach First and Teach for America, which were independent but sister organizations. The goal of Teach for All was to replicate their success globally. The essence of the programme was to get great graduates to teach in the most challenging schools. By 2024, Teach for All had developed a global network of 61 locally led and locally funded independent organizations, all devoted to the same mission.* It has succeeded by supporting local entrepreneurs who are committed to the mission and share the same values. Teach for All has avoided dependence on the founders of Teach First and Teach for America and it has also avoided trying to impose a 'one-size-fits-all' model around the world. Teach for All recognized that replication means adaptation to local conditions.

What works in one country rarely works exactly the same way in another. Even McDonald's adapts its menu by country to suit local tastes. Food is relatively simple, social systems are highly complex. You will need to adapt locally. This will force you to think very clearly about what is unique about your idea and what are the non-negotiable aspects of it. This in turn helps you focus on the magic sauce which is unique to you and your idea. Once you really understand your magic sauce, you can focus all your efforts and resources on building that.

The replication and scaling challenge is therefore also a focus challenge. Know what you are uniquely good at doing. The bigger your scale, the greater your focus must be in terms of scope and focus on that. In the private sector, the mantra is 'more with less'. Arguably the mantra in the not-for-profit sector should be 'less with more': focus on fewer activities and do them very well. If other organizations are

*https://teachforall.org/our-network#networkpartners

as good as you at an activity, partner with them and let them do it. Do not try to do it all yourself.

The sustainability challenge highlights a key difference between the private sector and the voluntary sector. In the private sector, scale is a blessing. In the voluntary sector, scale is a curse. In the private sector, size normally drives scale economies, which increases profitability and enables more investment. Scale is a success spiral which allows you to expand further and further. In the voluntary sector scale is a curse because it means you have to raise more money to stay afloat. The more you chase the money, the more likely you are to compromise your goals in order to keep your funders happy.

At startup, sustainability means making sure you meet payroll at the end of each month. In practice, you do not need to worry about the long-term sustainability challenge too much from day one. You need to focus on the short-term sustainability challenge. However, the long-term challenge will become more compelling and urgent over time as you grow.

If you start out with an effective, but high-cost model you may well demonstrate spectacular short-term results. For instance, Reach to Teach started out as an imaginative project to support education in some of the most marginalized rural communities in Gujarat, north-west India. Initially, it was seen to be a successful programme. But although successful, it was neither scalable nor sustainable. The average cost per child was reputed to be over $100 per year[*] in the early years of the programme. That may not sound much if you live in the USA, but in rural areas of India, average incomes for casual labourers are around $150 per month[†] and the most marginalized communities live on much less. This was a huge intervention by local standards. It could not address the global problem of roughly 300 million children

---

[*] The $100 figure came from a usually reliable source. It also gained traction as a nice round number on the NGO rumour mill, where it was widely quoted. It has not been independently verified.
[†] https://www.statista.com/statistics/1071788/india-average-daily-earnings-of-casual-laborer-rural-by-gender/

who are not receiving a decent education.* Scaling Reach to Teach globally would cost over $30 billion annually. No one is going to fund that level of cost year after year. Even Larry Ellison, who provided initial support for Reach to Teach,† might find $30 billion a year leaves him with little pocket money.

At the end of 2017 a new CEO came into Reach to Teach who recognized the scaling challenge. Scale and impact remained important, especially with a major funder like Larry Ellison, who was unlikely to support local, low-level change. New CEO Steve Cutts changed direction. The only viable route to scale was to work with and through the Gujarat state government. Within two years, Gujarat adopted the principles which Reach to Teach had demonstrated and rolled it out to all 32,000 primary schools across the state. Reach to Teach continued to work in roughly 200 demonstration schools which showcased best practice and gave credibility to the recommendations of Reach to Teach. Without those schools, Reach to Teach would simply have become another consulting practice touting its ideas.

Scaling is rarely a straight-line exercise where you do more of the same. It usually requires creative thinking about how you can apply the lessons you learned during a pilot stage at scale. If you intend to work at national scale, it is hard to avoid working through government. You need to start building the core relationships and shaping your intervention with this in mind from the start.

If you have an idea which is expensive to start with, don't panic. In the first few years of operation, you are simply testing and refining your idea. During this time you can work out how to reduce the cost of your idea so that it becomes scalable and sustainable.

---

*United Nations Sustainable Development Goal 4 estimates that by 2030, 300 million children will leave education without the basic literacy and numeracy skills to cope with modern life. https://sdgs.un.org/goals/goal4#progress_and_info
†https://www.reach-to-teach.org/our-work/

Is your idea different and/or better than existing programmes?
The students were in their sophomore year at a Midwestern university. They were sitting in the grounds of a hotel in Kampala and were very excited. For most of them, it was the first time that they had been outside the United States, so this was a big adventure. They were in Kampala on behalf of a small charity which got volunteers to teach in some schools in northern Uganda over their vacation period. Clearly, this was going to be a hugely valuable and formative experience for the students from the Midwest. It was less clear what the Ugandan schools got out of it, beyond some extra funding to pay for much-needed textbooks.

There are countless small charities raising money for volunteer work, for textbooks, for clothing and for the other myriad needs which exist in Uganda and beyond. Invariably, they do not have the resources to measure if they are having an impact. Nor do they know how they fit with the work of other initiatives: they may support, or overlap or undermine other programmes and may leave gaps of need unfilled. These are interventions which are welcome at a local level, but have neither the ambition nor the ability to go to a system scale: they have no idea how they fit with the whole system and no desire to fit with the whole system.

Going across the border into Rwanda, we found an entirely different situation. In Uganda, the officials were welcoming to most ideas and interventions. If you wanted to help, you could help as you saw fit, within reason. The Rwandan government was less laissez-faire and more structured and directed. Before we did anything with the government, they wanted to make sure it fitted with their national agenda. Even then, they wanted to make sure we did not duplicate existing work and that we had an offering which was genuinely high quality with impact. The government was not interested in receiving random acts of kindness.

The programme we were leading was about raising English language proficiency in schools, for both teachers and students. This was a relevant impact, because in 2008 Rwanda had made the spectacular decision to change its official language overnight

21

from French to English: an entire nation had to learn a new official language. Although our impact was relevant to Rwanda's need, the government still wanted to make sure it was differentiated and fit with existing programmes. The government had plenty of providers who were happy to work in the capital, Kigali, and a few larger towns. They had few resources addressing the language challenge in the countryside, where most people live. That is where we were directed to focus our efforts.

From an NGO's perspective, it is far easier to work in Uganda than in Rwanda with the result that many more NGOs work there. But from a system perspective, it may be that fewer is better. By integrating and focusing the work of NGOs around a national agenda, Rwanda can get more impact per dollar of NGO investment.

You should not have to rely on government to tell you if your idea is relevant and different or better than existing programmes. You should be able to tell the government how your idea works with their needs and with existing offerings. Just as in the private sector, you need to do your market research: work out what the customer needs are and what the competitive offerings are. Only work where you are relevant to the customer and you are different or better than competition.

Does your idea attract great people?
Venture capitalists do not just back a great idea, they back a great entrepreneur. Great people and great ideas go together like a needle and thread or a hammer and nail. The idea and the people depend on each other and improve each other. A great idea will get the most out of great people, who will make the idea even better. The only way you will build your fledgling idea into a great idea is to talk to lots of people: friends, colleagues, experts, practitioners and anyone else who will give you the time of day.

In starting Teach First, we talked to everyone we could find. We did not realize it at the time, but we were not just correcting flaws and improving the original idea: we were slowly building a coalition for change. Inevitably, there were sceptics. We could hear the air being sucked over their gums as they asked unhelpful questions such as 'how do you think your young graduates are going to master, in just six weeks of training, the 57 skills teachers normally acquire in two years?' and 'are you sure it is ethical to let graduates teach after so little training?' These questions were like a cancer of doubt, but for every cynic who saw problems, there were optimists who saw solutions. They were the coalition of the willing who selected themselves onto our team, our board and our supporters' groups.

You will inevitably get rejections and the more you talk, the more you will be challenged. That is healthy. Constructive challenges will help you adapt and improve your idea. Negative challenges will alert you to who is likely to resist your idea and why: you will be able to prepare your defences accordingly. The only really destructive response is indifference. If key stakeholders shout at you, at least that shows they are engaged. It gives you the chance to work with them and occasionally your greatest opponent can become your greatest champion. But if they are indifferent, it shows they just do not care. Indifference is far deadlier to your idea than opposition.

Some social entrepreneurs fear that someone will steal your idea. They won't. People are too busy with their own lives; they do not have the time to develop their own rival idea and they probably do not want to take on all the risk and uncertainty of a new startup. They will be delighted to talk to you, because it is flattering to be consulted. But the leap from talking to doing is one that few people make. They will be more than happy for you to take the lead.

At the idea stage, the sorts of great people you need include:

- Funders who will give you money. In the early days, even a few thousand dollars makes all the difference.
- Experts and stakeholders who can improve your idea and help you avoid pitfalls.
- Potential colleagues who might want to work with you to start up your new venture. You will need a mix of high skills (e.g. finance, monitoring and evaluation) and high values: energy, optimism, adaptability and a strong work ethic.

- Influencers and power brokers who can provide you with access to the right people, including funders and policy makers: you will draw your initial board from these people, if they have the right values.
- Policy makers and government officials: most change-the-world ideas will, eventually, need to work with governments. It pays to have officials on board from an early stage.

This list looks like a lot of conversations and appearances do not deceive: you will spend a long time setting up meetings, gaining access and having conversations. Many will go nowhere, a few will lead to breakthroughs. These are conversations you can have while you are doing your day job. If the conversations lead you to believe your idea will not fly, you have lost nothing but learned much. If your conversations attract great people and polish your idea, then you know you can leave your day job with greatly reduced risk.

Finally, do not worry if your idea meets with rejection. Yunus repeatedly attempted to get the banks to take up his idea and expand it. They kept on putting up obstacles and ever more difficult requirements for him to prove that his idea was sound in practice.

- Initially, the banks refused to provide credit to the poor because they were not seen to be credit worthy, even though Yunus could show that they were repaying his loans in full.
- Then the banks insisted that he should show that his idea could work far away from Jobra or Chittagong: they assumed that repayment was only happening because of his personal standing in the community. The bankers chose Tangail for the test district: near to them, and far from him. The test worked as it had done in Jobra.
- Then the banks argued that the Tangail test only worked because Yunus was personally involved so he agreed to do a test in five different districts: he could not be in five different districts at the same time.

- Even after the five-district test succeeded, the banks still rejected the idea. Yunus now realized that they just did not want to lend to the poor. Banks prefer to lend money to people who have money, not to those who lack money.

Throughout this process of constant rejection, Yunus was proving his idea and showing how it could work in practice and at scale. Constant rejection helped him build the confidence to apply to the central bank for a banking licence to start his own bank, Grameen Bank. If the established banks had taken over his idea, it would have died through neglect: it would never have been a priority for them. Rejection was the route to success, as it has been for countless entrepreneurs and artists through the ages.

TEACH FIRST: WHEN 'NO' IS SIMPLY A PRELUDE TO 'YES'

The meeting with the minister had been set up for him to bless the new venture and agree initial funding. Our business supporters came to the meeting to share our collective triumph. The minister arrived late and after some tense pleasantries said, 'I'm sorry, this idea just won't run. Too risky. But thank you for all your efforts.'

The civil servants vanished and our business backers could not be seen for dust as they ran off. Just Brett Wigdortz and I were left. I turned to Brett and said: 'It's OK: a "no" is simply a prelude to a "yes": let's work out how to get to the "yes".'

Had we accepted the minister's words at face value, we would have re-worked our idea to show that it was a 100 per cent guaranteed success, but we knew enough to realize that nothing is as it seems in government so we talked to everyone we could, again. Slowly, we found the truth: the risk was not that the idea would fail, the real risk was that the idea would succeed. If it succeeded, that would embarrass the minister because it would show that his expensive graduate recruitment programme was

---

a complete failure. Only in government can an idea get rejected because it might succeed.

So we arranged another meeting with the minister. This time we showed that Teach First would make a very modest contribution and that it would have no overlap with his scheme. This was a shameless lie, but it worked. He backed the idea, it was a great success and within two years his scheme was closed down. By then, Teach First was 'his' project and we were happy for him to claim the credit.

Great ideas attract great opposition: rejection by vested interests is normal and healthy. Rejection shows that you are challenging conventional practice. Far from being discouraged by rejection, you should feel emboldened by it.

CHANGING THE WORLD AND MAKING MONEY

Throughout history the world has been changed by people in pursuit of making money. This has often been catastrophic. The Conquistadors made fortunes by conquering the Aztec and Inca empires: Europe got silver, potatoes and tomatoes while the indigenous people got Catholicism, slavery and disease, which wiped them out. But it does not have to be like that. The Victorian era mixed the good, the bad and the ugly. There were countless economic abuses, but also great enlightenment. The Quakers in particular built model businesses and model towns which sought to nurture, not to exploit their workers. The Cadburys at Bournville are a classic example. Their product, chocolate, was an antidote to the vice of alcohol as they saw it. In 1893, George Cadbury bought 120 acres of land near his factory and built, at his own expense, a model village which would 'alleviate the evils of modern, more cramped living conditions'. This included not just generous housing, but also schools and medical facilities: it was a mini welfare state.

More recently, the world has been changed dramatically by the tech revolution: Apple, Microsoft, Google and Facebook have their problems but few people want to turn the clock back to an era when none of them existed. Even firms which have no obvious moral purpose can make a positive difference. Financial firms are often reviled as amoral money grubbers, but a world without insurance or banking would not work. We need such firms, and we need them to work in an ethical manner: doing good and making money are not mutually exclusive.

FOR-PROFIT OR NOT-FOR-PROFIT?

Buffy Price worked for many years in the not-for-profit sector: animal welfare, Amnesty, politics and sustainable development. She then switched to the for-profit sector: why would someone do that?

Buffy realized that she could make a large and positive impact working in the for-profit sector. She is the co-founder of Carbon Re, which uses AI to help cement producers reduce their energy usage and carbon emissions. Cement producers are major carbon emitters. Many have little interest in reducing emissions but great interest in reducing costs. Carbon Re helps them achieve both. A not-for-profit advocacy group would be unlikely to succeed by appealing to the better instincts of the producers; Carbon Re can help them and make a profit at the same time.

Price also found other advantages to the for-profit sector. Decision making is much easier: the profit goal simplifies priorities. Mission driven organizations operate in a grey space of bureaucracy, democratic decision making and uncertainty over how best to allocate resources. The profit sector also let Carbon Re raise $8 million venture capital investment to grow, which would have been inconceivable in the not-for-profit sector. Growth is much more sustainable in the for-profit sector, if you can get your service offering right.

So which is best: not-for-profit or for-profit?

Developing your idea is the same process in both the for-profit and not-for-profit sectors. There is rarely one light-bulb moment when the whole idea springs to life in an instant. Instead, there are endless discussions as the idea develops and the coalition of success is built. This is how Tortoise Media came to challenge the way traditional media work. Tortoise Media was set up by Matthew Harding, Katie Vanneck-Smith and Matthew Barzun in 2019. Instead of instant news, they look at deep news: they find out why things are happening and how they are shaping the world instead of just reporting on who has done what, where and when. And they are building a new economic model, based on membership which drives deeper engagement with their community. They are re-thinking media in a bold experiment which could change the world. Making money is the only way they can sustain and grow their idea: money is the fuel of change.

If you want to change the world, the for-profit route can be highly attractive. You can scale your idea more easily because you can borrow money and make profits to re-invest in it. You break free from the vagaries of funders with endless different requirements; instead, you subject yourself to the disciplines of the market. Market discipline is simple and useful: if something works, you do more of it; if something does not work, you change it or stop it. Market feedback is quick and you can change or scale fast in response. In contrast, messages from funders are often much more mixed and ambiguous because they all have different needs and perspectives. In the absence of clear market signals, it is much harder for NGOs to learn, change and scale at speed.

As a for-profit firm you have an investment advantage over NGOs. You can invest in people, IT, test markets, training, proper financial systems and all the other corporate life-support systems that enable success. In the not-for-profit sector, funders are reluctant to fund any of this because they regard corporate life-support systems as wasteful overhead. It is very hard for NGOs to acquire sufficient free reserves to make the investments they need. Funders who provide unre-stricted funding are like gold dust.

Choosing between the for-profit and not-for-profit route is often framed as an ethical issue. If you really want to change the world, frame the issue as a question of scalability, sustainability and impact.

IDEA: SUMMARY

You need neither money nor expertise to change the world. The best ideas start with little or no money, and often start with outsiders who see things differently. You do not need to be a genius to find your idea. Your great idea can come from:

- Hearing an idea through the media or friends and adapting it
- Encountering a problem and trying to solve it, by iterating your way to the best solution.

Here are four tests of your idea:

1. What is your impact?
   - Random acts of kindness do more harm than good: understand your impact properly.
   - Are you providing temporary relief from a problem (palliative care, disaster relief)? These are needed but will not change the world.
   - Are you focused on the symptom or the cause of a problem? Symptoms are easy to address and measure impact, but do not fix the problem.
2. Is your idea scalable, replicable and sustainable?
   - Scaling means building a delivery machine which does not depend on the inspiration and charisma of the founders.
   - Replication means adapting to local conditions: that forces you to focus on your magic sauce, which must be constant across geographies.
   - Sustainability financially is easier for private firms (economies of scale) than for NGOs which have to chase the money, risking loss of focus on the core mission.

3. Is your idea different and/or better than existing programmes?
- Changing the world normally requires system change: understand how you fit into making system change, work with partners and government.
- If your idea replicates existing provision, then why do it? Do your competitive and market research.
- Someone else is probably already working on your problem, if it is significant. If it was easy to fix your challenge, someone would have done it already. Don't be discouraged by competition.

4. Does it attract great people?
- Big ideas attract more attention, support and opposition than small ideas.
- Opposition is good: it shows you that your idea is taken seriously and it helps you refine your idea.
- The quality of your idea improves with the quality of the people you attract.

Finally, you can change the world and make a profit. What matters is changing the world.

2

Impact

Adapt your idea so that it has impact at scale

If you want to change the world, you need to have impact. The impact needs to be at scale. Having an impact on your local community is wonderful, but global impact requires global scale. This chapter looks at the challenges of impact and scale.

- *Why scale matters – and why it is dangerous*
- *Think big, start small, scale fast*
- *Five routes to scale*
- *Scale or scope?*
- *Measuring your impact.*

WHY SCALE MATTERS – AND WHY IT IS DANGEROUS

Global impact requires global scale, which is why I found myself driving across the Sahara to Timbuktu, which exotically symbolizes the middle of nowhere. It is situated at the northern most point of the River Niger, making it the perfect trading post for caravans crossing the Sahara. Salt caravans come from Mauretania and all sorts make their way north to the Mediterranean: some of the trade is even reputed to be legal. The local Tuareg have been traders and raiders since time immemorial. They are born survivors who neither want nor need the help of government or anyone else.

As I approached Timbuktu, I started to see a series of metal hoardings by the side of the road. Each one proclaimed the presence of another NGO. Their presence was then confirmed by monstrous 4 x 4 vehicles with outsized antennas roaring along the narrow tarmac strip. There was no need for so many NGOs to be in such a remote place. Although remote, Timbuktu was relatively safe and prosperous at the time, with many ancient Islamic libraries testifying to its cultural importance.

The NGOs were not there for the sake of Timbuktu, they were there for their own sake. They were planting the flag, like latter-day colonialists with a moral mission. Like colonialists, they had their own clubs and bars where they could relax, away from the gaze of the locals. The NGOs wanted to show to their funders that they could reach the most remote places on earth. The funders had no real idea whether Timbuktu needed help or not, but it sounds suitably remote and exotic to merit some form of intervention.

'Planting the flag' is a classic sign of an NGO which has lost its way. Scale and reach become a substitute for impact and mission. The more they scale, the more they have to chase the money to fund their ambitions. They land up doing what their funders want, rather than focusing on their mission.

Scale is not an end in itself. And scaling is positively dangerous if you do not have a clear model of how you are going to have impact at scale. The way you have impact in a local community is different from how you will have impact globally. At a local level, you can rely much more on the power of your personal intervention and on high effort and goodwill from volunteers. At a global level you need to think differently: you need systemic interventions. In all likelihood you will have to work with governments and large partner organizations: this means you have less direct control over your impact. You rely less on the power of personality and more on the power of partnerships and a strong delivery machine.

None of this will be obvious when you start out. When you start, all that matters is that you find a way of achieving the impact you want. Once you have done that, you have to start thinking about how to achieve the same impact at scale.

Inevitably, this means that the first few years will be as much about learning as they are about delivery. This is a really tough message both for you and for your funders. The natural inclination is to focus on, and to measure, the impact you are having. And if you have some good results, you will be under pressure to expand the programme. But, as we saw with the example of Reach to Teach, what works at small scale may not be economic at a global scale. You have to work out a different way of delivering the same impact, but at a fraction of the cost. And you need to work with funders who understand that short-term impact is a waste of money: the real investment is in learning how to deliver at scale.

In your first few years of operation, you face a paradox that to be truly ambitious you have to be truly humble. Real ambition is not about changing a few communities, it is about changing the world. But then you need real humility to recognize that what is working in a few communities will not work at global scale. Instead of scaling your success model, you have to spend years learning how to build a new model which will work at scale.

To illustrate the challenge of impact at scale, we will look at the evolution of STIR Education. STIR addresses the UN challenge that there are 300 million children in school but not learning. This is clearly a global scale challenge, which STIR recognized from the start: a quiet conversation over a cup of tea.

Absent or inadequate teachers were widely seen as the problem for the 300 million children. The reaction was to use traditional carrots and sticks, including biometric scanners to check teachers in and out of school. STIR challenged this narrative. First, it saw teachers as the solution, not the problem: great education requires great teachers. Second, STIR believed the way to address the problem was to help teachers re-engage: help them rediscover their intrinsic motivation for teaching. If the teachers are intrinsically motivated, they will turn up without having to clock on and off; they will be motivated to improve their teaching mastery and they will motivate the children to learn.

This germ of an idea took seven years and multiple iterations to reach scale. The STIR story below reflects a few basic principles of scaling:

- You need to keep changing and adapting your idea as it grows. Don't fall in love with your original idea: drop it or adapt it as you need.
- Focus on scaling the mission: scaling the organization is ineffective and uneconomic.
- Stay true to your mission: do not chase the money if that means changing your focus.
- Be prepared to work at a system level with major partners and governments who have the capacity to deliver at scale. Partnership working is vital to scale.
- Find funders who are ready to act as your patient partners and understand that they are investing to learn what works at global scale.
- Be humble to be ambitious: know that you do not know all the answers. You need to discover what works and find good partners who will support you on your journey of discovery.
- More scale means more focus: strip your idea down to its bare essentials. This is your 'magic sauce', which you should take to scale. The bigger you are, the less you do: focus makes your idea affordable at scale.

STIR EDUCATION AND THE REALITY OF TAKING AN IDEA TO GLOBAL SCALE

STIR 1.0. Pilot and micro-innovations with individual teachers
STIR started in 2011 with some private schools in Delhi and Uganda, simply because they were easier to access than working through the state system. The intervention was to ask teachers to identify micro-innovations which they could share with colleagues to improve teaching and learning.

STIR 2.0. Testing structured whole school impact
STIR made three major shifts:

- Shifted to the State system, away from private schools. At scale, it is easier to serve state schools than private schools.
- Opened in another state: Uttar Pradesh.
- Adapted the intervention so that it focused on teachers holding structured workshops to help each other improve their practice.

Behind these radical changes, much remained the same:

- The mission was unchanged: help 300 million children get a decent education.
- Belief that teachers are the solution, not the problem, remained the same.
- Belief that intrinsic motivation of teachers is the key to unlocking their success remained the same.

These guiding beliefs remained constant on the whole STIR journey.

STIR 3.0 Testing system solutions
STIR realized that the motivation of teachers depended on the motivation and support of the whole system: cluster, district, state and national officials needed to support teachers. They also needed to rediscover their intrinsic motivation as many officials found they spent more time doing administrative work, rather than supporting good education.

In this iteration, STIR expanded again to three more states in India. It used expansion to re-set expectations that STIR was a whole system intervention. It worked with government officials all the way from the schools minister down to individual teachers. During this time it declined offers of major funding to expand to other countries. It wanted to work out how to achieve impact at a system level before expanding into unfamiliar systems.

STIR 4.0 Testing global scale solutions

STIR is expanding again to Indonesia and Brazil. Instead of taking the lead in making system change, it is working through government and NGO partners to change the system itself. This has a dramatic impact on costs. STIR 1.0 cost about $4 per child. To scale that to support 300 million children would cost $1.2 billion a year, which is just impractical. It would also be ineffective, because STIR would own the programme, not the system. STIR was clear that if change is to be effective, it has to be done *by* the system not *to* the system. Instead of scaling STIR the organization, it is focused on scaling the mission by getting governments to embed the STIR approach in their education systems. This stage could only be reached once the intervention had become stabilized through extensive testing in stages 1.0 to 3.0.

The current STIR cost per child is now under 30 cents per child, which is closer to a globally scalable solution. The rest of the costs are born by the sponsoring government. In practice, they have minimal extra costs: most of the cost is about redirecting existing labour effort.

STIR 4.0 is more or less unrecognizable from STIR 1.0, but the mission and the beliefs remain the same. Reaching STIR 4.0 required seven years of constant learning, organizational agility and endless patience from funders and supporters. Behind this apparently smooth progression to scale, there were predictable and unpredictable crises, challenges in scaling the organization, challenges in finding the right partners and inevitably, mistakes were made. You need both agility and resilience to sustain the discovery journey.

FIVE ROUTES TO SCALE

There are five main routes to scale. These are not mutually exclusive: you will probably need to use some combination of all five. These five routes are:

1. Scale the organization organically (direct control)
2. Scale the organization through mergers and acquisitions (direct control)
3. Replicate the organization globally (direct control)
4. Build a movement (indirect control)
5. Work through partnerships (indirect control).

Inevitably, most people feel most comfortable where they have direct control. Scaling the organization and replication are popular strategies. They are also the most expensive ways of going to scale. The simplest way to estimate this cost is to look at the number of people you want to reach and the average cost of reaching them. This will tell you how much your idea will cost at global scale. In practice, you have to take your idea to scale by working through other people. You will need to develop a strong set of skills around managing and influencing stakeholders and partners you do not control. Do it well and you can achieve impact at global scale fast. Do it poorly and your idea will be wrecked by well-meaning partners who do not have your level of passion, expertise or commitment to make the idea work properly.

Here, we will briefly explore each of these options. They look like the sort of neat and easy options you will see on a PowerPoint presentation but in reality, any route to scale is messy. The journey to scale is a journey of discovery, because you cannot design the future on a simple PowerPoint presentation. The story of the Skills Builder Partnership (below), which is changing the nature of skills education in England, is a good example of how challenging and rewarding the journey can be. As you work your way through the scaling options, keep on learning and adapting because that is the only way you will discover your success model.

THE JOURNEY TO SCALE: SKILLS BUILDER PARTNERSHIP*

The Skills Builder Partnership started as a project in a single school in 2008. From there, it has gone through at least five major transformations until it has become the common language about how schools think about skills within a knowledge-based curriculum.

Stage 1: first ideas in response to a pressing problem. Nurturing the idea as a side hustle
As a new teacher in 2008, Tom was teaching a BTEC course, often an uninspiring way for pupils to secure a basic qualification. He was worried that his students weren't building any of the broader employability skills that they really needed.

Tom started by getting his students to do something useful. They began learning about enterprise by setting up enterprises including an in-school tutoring service, doughnut distribution, a wholesale alternative to the unpopular canteen. He shared his idea with other Teach First teachers and the idea spread so he then set up the social enterprise as a side hustle. Although he had no great master plan, he found it started to consume all his energy. He was feeling his way to success. He wanted to see if the idea was viable.

Stage 2: back to the drawing board. Start all over again
In 2010 the government changed the qualifications system, so Tom had to reinvent his model. He tried everything: after-school clubs, school projects, one-to-one lessons and any other way of earning money to stay afloat. He also started to raise money and his first grant of £10k seemed huge at the time. This was a challenging stage.

*Original interview with the founder, Tom Ravenscroft. The author is on the Advisory Board of the Skills Builder Partnership.

Stage 3: discovering the success model
It took another three or four years to find the success formula and have the courage to focus on it. They dropped projects and entrepreneurship (the original model) and focused on just eight essential skills: listening, presenting, problem solving, creativity, staying positive, aiming high, leadership and teamwork.

Having found the model, Tom and the team invested heavily in refining it so that it could be delivered all the way from reception class to the final year of school.

Stage 4: scaling the organization
It took Tom nearly ten years to discover the success model. Since 2016, the focus has been on taking the idea to scale. In his words: 'We did not have credibility from networks. We did not know the right people, so we had to demonstrate success to scale. We were really ambitious.'

As with developing the idea, Tom and the team had to iterate constantly to find the delivery model which could scale sustainably. This meant getting both the organization and economics right. The plan was to get schools to fund the programme and donors to fund investment in capacity and new ideas. Skills Builder was still scaling mainly through direct delivery.

Stage 5: scaling the mission, not the organization
COVID19 and a big squeeze on school budgets meant that they needed to find a new way of going to scale. The solution was to get other people to deliver the programme for them. In 2020, Tom and his team created the Skills Builder Universal Framework, which anyone can take and use anywhere in the world for free. By 2024 it was being used by 900 partner organizations around the world. It reaches over 2.6 million pupils. They achieved scale through partnership far faster than by scaling their own organization.

By moving to a partnership model, with indirect control, Skills Builder had to rethink its role. Instead of plain vanilla delivery, it adds huge value in different ways:

- Providing training and support in the Framework to partners
- Building partnerships with large corporates to deliver internships and other extra value
- Continuing research into the effects of the programme on both skills and knowledge
- Identifying and spreading best practice and innovative approaches.

All of this is achieved with a staff of about 30 people. Great impact does not require a great deal of people.

1. Scale the organization organically

This is a highly popular route with nearly everyone. Founders often equate scale with success. Governments find it easier to contract with large and mediocre organizations than with small and innovative ones. For staff, scale means more career opportunities and for board members, scale means more prestige and more bragging rights at dinner party conversations.

There are some very important benefits to scaling the organization. In practice, you will have to scale your organization to some extent if you are to achieve your mission. But scaling is only part of the solution. If scaling is the only solution, you will destroy and not deliver your mission. The main benefits of scaling are:

- *It is easier to hire well-qualified staff.* Smaller charities may hire entrepreneurial individuals who work hard and make a difference, but small charities lack the resources or career structure to hire people with deep experience and technical knowledge. As charities grow, it invariably becomes much easier to attract great talent.
- *Scale allows for more specialization and focus.* In the early days of any startup, the founder does everything from fundraising to being the HR manager, bookkeeper and IT specialist. It is hopelessly inefficient. With scale, charities can afford to hire

more specialist staff, freeing up everyone to focus on doing what they are best at doing.

- *Scale allows for more and better learning.* A small charity might run one or two projects and lack the resources to do an adequate evaluation of either of them. A larger charity might be running projects in 100 districts: each one can be a rich source of learning, innovation and experimentation. And the larger charity should have the resources to put in formal evaluation and assessment systems so that they can learn what works best and how to improve fast.

- *Large donors and governments prefer to work with large NGOs.* No government wants to integrate the work of 100 innovative small charities. It needs a few large, reliable partners who can deliver at scale on its behalf. Larger NGOs simply have the chance to bid for more work than smaller NGOs.

But scale is not a panacea. Scaling your organization may make it impossible to achieve your mission: the costs of growth will be unsustainable. The main problems of scaling are:

- *Achieving the mission may be impossible.* Even low-cost interventions become uneconomic if taken to full scale. STIR education found that spending as little as $4 per year per child was impossible if it was to serve 300 million children. It may not be financially possible to achieve your mission by growing the organization.

- *The organization loses mission focus.* Instead, the executive has to focus on scale, which means chasing the money and bending to the wants and needs of funders. The result is slow mission creep and loss of focus.

- *Staff motivation changes.* In a small organization, your staff will be very focused on the mission because you probably cannot pay them well or offer them much of a career path. A strong sense of mission is your main competitive point of difference in the war for talent. In a larger organization, staff are more likely to see your organization as a career move: they will be interested in getting the right experiences, development, salary and support. The mission of the organization will take second place to their personal mission of having a good career.

- *Scale leads to inefficiency.* Every organization swears that it will not become inefficient, slow and bureaucratic as it grows. Every organization follows the same trajectory: inefficiency, expense, slow decision making and bureaucracy creeps in. Economies of scale are offset by the inefficiencies of scale.

2. Scale the organization through mergers and acquisitions
The ultimate form of partnership between two organizations is when they merge. But mergers are both rare and difficult to achieve. In 2023 there were just 48 mergers involving 96 charities out of 169,000 charities in the UK.* That was a fairly typical year for mergers.

There are two reasons why charity mergers are rare: law and egos.

- *Law:* unlike the private sector, there is no market for corporate control: you cannot buy the shares of a target charity and take it over. Charitable legal structures make contested mergers and takeovers impossible: both parties have to consent willingly.
- *Egos:* most charities fiercely protect their independence. Many potential mergers fail because neither of the chairs or CEOs want to step down and make way for the other side to take control. Since the board and trustees effectively 'own' the charity, there is no way to take control without their consent.

The few mergers which do happen tend to be closer to takeovers than mergers: normally, the merger happens because one charity has run

*Eastside People publishes the Good Merger Index every year. https://eastsidepeople.org/resource/charity-good-merger-index-22-23-report/

into financial difficulty and needs the support of a stronger charity in the same area. Even then, egos can get in the way of survival. In one case, we organized the rescue of a charity which had lost its main contract with government, which accounted for 70 per cent of its revenues. It was losing money and using up its precious reserves. Despite this, the chair refused to agree to the rescue: she pointed out endless obstacles to the merger package, none of which seemed very rational. I then asked the chair of the failing charity, for which she was responsible, if she would like to chair the newly merged charity. Within 24 hours all the apparently insurmountable obstacles she had been raising vanished into thin air and the merger was back on.

Rescue mergers can be thought of as 1+1=1.5: two charities are merged, then overhead is stripped out and a leaner combined charity can survive. The merged charity turns out to be leaner and smaller than the two charities were separately, hence 1+1= 1.5.

The ideal sort of merger is 1+1 = 3: combine two charities to create something which can do more than the two organizations could do individually. This rare sort of merger happened when Teaching Leaders merged with Future Leaders. Teaching Leaders developed middle leaders for schools; Future Leaders developed head teachers for schools. Both had good products and both were partial solutions to the challenge of professional development in schools in disadvantaged areas. The two charities came together to form a brand new organization called Ambition Institute. It did not just combine the two charities to remove overhead duplication (for instance, IT, HR and finance), it changed the way it worked with schools. Instead of offering two products, it could offer complete bespoke solutions to schools. Ambition developed a suite of products to meet all the school's professional development needs. This suite could be customized to the different needs of each school. Ambition stopped being a normal vendor selling products to schools; instead it developed school relationships where they could offer complete solutions.

Even when you have agreed the merger in principle, you will face the challenges of merger integration. These are even harder than in the private sector. The private sector typically has more money to fix problems and to pay off staff where needed. The profit motive also provides a clear rationale for decision making. In a charity, you do not have the luxury of funding to pay for expensive merger integration projects; you cannot fund consultants to come in and integrate your IT systems; you cannot just pay people off. Decision making is hard because there will always be arguments about which activities best support the mission and how the mission should be interpreted. The mission does not give the same simple decision making clarity as the profit motive.

The ultimate form of merger is to 'sell' your idea to government. Once government adopts your idea as policy, you are guaranteed scale and funding. You will not be guaranteed the quality and passion that you brought with the idea but the success of your idea should not depend on your personal passion. If it is to be scalable and sustainable, it needs to be delivered reliably by a strong machine. In most wealthy countries, the strongest and most pervasive machine belongs to the government.

This approach represents one of the best ways in which social enterprises can change the world. They can act as the social research lab for government, testing and building ideas which are simply too risky for government to do themselves. Most governments have a poor record of useful innovation: your social enterprise can help plug that gap. Find an idea, test and develop it and then get government to take it over.

For instance, Michael (Lord) Young believed there had to be a better way of delivering health advice nationally. GP surgeries are often over-booked and are only open during week days. Out-of-hours service was becoming harder to access which meant that many people were resorting to going to Accident and Emergency (A&E) units at hospitals. This overwhelmed A&E services, putting at risk patients who had real emergencies while causing huge delays for other people wanting treatment or advice.

Young's solution was to set up a telephone support service to offer free advice over the phone for people who did not really need A&E but could not access a GP. This was not the sort of idea government would want to try out: offering medical advice without being able to see the patient or do any tests seemed like a recipe for disaster. But Young believed it could work, which would give him a headache because if it worked, demand for the service would explode and he did not have the resources to fund a national programme at scale so his intention was always to prove the concept and get government to take it over.

Young's service started out as Healthline. It was eventually adopted by government in 1998 and went through several changes (NHS Choices, NHS Direct) until it became the NHS 111 non-emergency number. Now it receives up to 2 million calls per month,* providing timely advice to patients and relieving pressure on A&E departments and GPs. Young successfully scaled the idea, not the organization.

3. Replicate the organization

Most charities start off locally, which means that the most direct way to scale is to replicate the service in other locations, nationally or internationally. This is a good test of whether you have a sound model. Replication forces you to build a machine which can deliver results without your close attendance. If success depends on you personally weaving your magic, you do not have a model which will change the world. Your NGO needs to thrive without you.

When Yunus started his poverty alleviation programme in Bangladesh, the banks were quite right to test him by asking him to replicate his model elsewhere, and preferably in multiple areas. They had to be convinced that the model did not depend on Yunus's social standing in the community, or his personal efforts. He showed that microfinancing worked as a replicable model by starting programmes in five locations at the same time: even Yunus has not mastered the art of omnipresence, so this was a great test of microfinance for the

---

*https://www.nuffieldtrust.org.uk/resource/nhs-111. In January 2024, NHS 111 received 1.9 million calls. Demand has overwhelmed the service, with only 53 per cent of calls being answered within 60 seconds.

poorest in society. It is to his credit that the test worked and to the shame of the banks that they chose to ignore the test so that they could focus on lending money to people who do not need it, or need it less. Now that Yunus's Grameen Bank has over 10 million borrowing members in Bangladesh, he has proven the power of replicating a strong model in village after village.

Replication is a highly attractive model which works well in the private sector. Coca-Cola, Starbucks and McDonald's are all built on replicating a strong model globally. Although every country claims it is unique, these formulas have proved fairly universal much to the surprise of many locals. If you really want to annoy a French gastronome, invite her out to France's favourite restaurant and watch her face as you enter McDonald's: 'favourite' does not always mean 'best'. But even these ubiquitous global brands are not entirely homogenous. For instance, you might be surprised to go into your local McDonald's* and find the following on the menu:

- Teriyaki Burger, Shaka Shaka chicken, Ebi (shrimp) filet-o (Tokyo)
- Crispy chicken with rice, Chicken with McSpaghetti (Manila)
- McSpicy Paneer Supreme, McAloo Tikki, Masala Grill Veg (Delhi)

The reality is that no formula translates seamlessly across all borders. This is especially true for interventions in social systems which are unique in each country. In most countries you will be able to generate demand for fries and Coca-Cola. But that is completely different to working out how to address the challenges of education, or poverty and the environment in each country. The challenges and the context vary too much for a single formula to work consistently well across borders.

---

*You can see all the local variations of McDonald's menus by going to their local websites.

GOING GLOBAL: *SESAME STREET**

The TV series *Sesame Street* started out in 1969 in America as an educational programme for pre-schoolers. It has since evolved to the point where over 150 million children see it every week in 150 countries around the world.

Sesame Street lacked the in-house knowledge to understand how to replicate its model into other countries. Instead of replicating directly, it works with 39 co-producers around the world. Each co-production adheres to the core principles of *Sesame Street*:

- Help build literacy, numeracy, social and emotional wellbeing, and health knowledge and practice in early childhood.
- Follow a universal style and format, but with unique characters, content and media.
- Extensively test ideas and adapt accordingly: *Sesame Street* has conducted over 10,000 evaluations, making it perhaps the most researched NGO intervention globally.

Sesame Street's expansion has been through a flexible form of replication. TV programmes made for children watching television in the Midwest are unlikely to work in the slums of Nairobi or Delhi. The challenge is not just with the content. Television is not a good way of reaching disadvantaged groups in India: they will not only lack television, they may also lack electricity. That meant that *Sesame Street* would become an intervention for relatively privileged and wealthy children only, unless it could find a way of reaching hard-to-reach groups. The Indian version of *Sesame Street*, known as *Galli Galli Sim Sim* in Hindi, came up with a unique local solution. They repurposed old vegetable carts, added a TV and DVD player and sent them into the alleys of the slums with a facilitator. The facilitator would engage parents and children, and

*Christina Kwauk, Daniela Petrova and Jenny Perlman Robinson, Center for Universal Education at Brookings, 2019.

ask the children content related questions to help them capture the learning from the shows.

Sesame Street started in India in 2006 as a co-production between Sesame Street and Turner Entertainment through Miditech, an Indian TV production company based in Gurgaon, which is just outside Delhi. This co-production approach lasted five years so that there could be a full transfer of the knowledge, format and values while at the same time working out what would, and would not, work in India.

The process of replication forces you to focus on what really matters to you. For *Sesame Street*, the original characters and story lines were not part of a universal secret sauce. What mattered was the underlying approach, backed up by rigorous analysis and testing, to allow the model to be adapted to local conditions. You cannot adapt your model until you deeply understand what the core of your model is.

4. Build a movement

The purpose of charities and NGOs is not to make a profit or to become a big organization. It is to achieve a mission: reducing poverty, improving health, education or the environment, for instance. If you are truly focused on the mission, you should want the best people to deliver it with the best solutions. Many founders look no further than the mirror when they look for the best person to deliver the mission. This is classic founder syndrome: you have done all the hard work to build an idea from scratch; you have overcome obstacles, opposition and indifference; you have shown that you can deliver. No one else has done what you have done so you are the natural person to deliver the mission globally. But in practice, there are plenty of reasons why you may not be the right person:

- The same mission requires vital variations in each country if it is to succeed. What worked in your home country will need translation. You cannot translate into every country around the world, just as you cannot speak every language in the world.

- If you lead the mission yourself, you will land up with a huge global organization and with all the problems that entails.
- Leading a large global organization requires very different skills from leading a modest national organization. You can no longer exert direct control over everything: you have to build a machine which can run the organization for you.
- You will start to suffer the downside of founder's syndrome. When you stay too long, hubris takes over. Hubris means you start to indulge in ever more grandiose ideas and ignore the humdrum basics of day-to-day operation. Hubris means that you start to believe in your own infallibility: you only listen to your own advice and top talent decides it wants to work elsewhere. Inevitably, nemesis follows hubris.
- There are many highly talented and committed people in the world. Some of them might even be able to deliver better than you can. And if you really believe in your mission, you should really believe in getting the best people to deliver it.

Instead of trying to change the world single-handed, find other people to do it for you. Build a movement of like-minded people who share your passion and purpose. Let them work out how to adapt your idea to different contexts around the world. This deals with the replication challenge. It also represents a trade-off: by adapting your idea locally you achieve replication but you also lose some control. By definition, any adaptation is a change to your original formula: this can be hard for a founder to accept.

In practice, you have to be clear about what your non-negotiables are. This means stripping your idea right back to its basics and focusing on what matters most. It's a useful exercise to do. It not only informs what replication globally should look like, it also helps refocus your efforts in your home market.

BUILDING A MOVEMENT: TEACH FOR ALL (TFA)

TFA started in 2007 as a partnership between Teach for America and Teach First. Both organizations came to share some common goals and values which provided the basis for starting TFA:

- Recruit top graduates and train them to become qualified teachers, at high speed;
- Place the teachers in areas of significant economic disadvantage which traditionally struggle to recruit teachers;
- Cultivate life-long leadership;
- Build partnerships with schools, communities and government;
- Believe that no child's prospects should be held back by where they were born.

These goals and values were adapted to become 'unifying principles' for the TFA network, which has now grown to 61 countries around the world. The network has grown organically by helping entrepreneurial individuals start their own version of TFA where they live. Even the name of the organization changes: Teach for Thailand, Teach First Deutschland, Le Choix de l'école (France), Lead for Ghana. Behind the different names lies a common goal, shared values and many shared methods.

The movement enables rapid scaling and replication. The local entrepreneur is able to approach government and funders with the credibility of a global network behind them. They also benefit from the global knowledge of what works and what does not; they gain access to global funders and direct support from TFA. This reduces risk and accelerates growth for the local entrepreneur.

TFA also enjoys reduced risk and accelerated progress: the local entrepreneur knows how best to adapt TFA to local conditions and is best placed to develop the local networks of support and government access, which are vital to success. The role of TFA is to provide the support to help the entrepreneurs get started and to facilitate learning across the network as a whole. This is light touch but very high impact.

TFA has built a global movement with relatively low resources: its annual revenues in 2023 were $55 million.* That supports a global annual investment of up to $1 billion a year in TFA partner programmes around the world. The TFA investment is leveraged even further by the substantial in-kind support from governments which normally fund the initial teacher training and fund the teachers' salaries.

Sometimes, the best way to succeed is by letting go. But letting go is the hardest thing for a founder to do. There are many versions of letting go and of building a movement, including licensing and franchising your idea. In practice, the most common method is to build a membership movement like TFA or the Scouts and Girl Guides. In each case, you have to focus on what are the core essentials of your programme and ensure that all members adhere to those essentials. You also need to be clear about what value you add to your members. For the Scouts, for instance, membership means access to the World Scout Jamboree held every four years and to many exchange and travel opportunities. In return, each member has to subscribe to the aims and values of the Scout Movement and in particular to refrain from any political activity. This is a formula which has worked for over 100 years, since the Scouts were formed in 1908. Today, there are now over 50 million Scouts in 170 countries worldwide.

In similar fashion, both the Rotary Club and the Lions Club have grown from modest Midwestern roots over 100 years ago. They have become global organizations with over a million members each, spread across tens of thousands of individual clubs. Both clubs allow significant autonomy to individual clubs who organize themselves and select their own members while adhering to the values and the

---

*https://projects.propublica.org/nonprofits/organizations/262122566

goals of the global club. Being part of a global club gives each local chapter credibility and cachet which it would not have if it was a stand-alone local organization. When you build a movement, the movement does all the hard work for you in terms of growth.

Building a movement forces you to focus clearly on what you most want to achieve and where you add most value. It is a good exercise for anyone to undertake.

5. Work through partnerships

However successful your charity, it will not provide a comprehensive solution to the challenge it is addressing. Poverty, disaster relief, health, environmental challenges, climate change are all beyond the scope of any one government, let alone any single charity. That means you will always be working in partnership with other organizations to achieve your mission, even if it is not an explicit partnership.

At its simplest level, you need to work out where you fit in amid all the different actors who are working towards the same goal. This means you need to be clear about your impact: how is it relevant to the mission and different to the other actors in the same space? For instance, STIR Education is very clear that it does not provide the whole solution to the UN challenge of 300 million children in school but not learning. Its distinctive contribution is to help teachers and officials at all levels rediscover their intrinsic motivation. STIR calls this 'preparing the soil' for other NGOs and other interventions. Other interventions can only work if teachers and officials are motivated to make them work. Putting in a literacy programme, however good, into a system where teachers and officials lack interest or motivation is a good way to lose money. This partnership is not explicit: no NGO has to sign up to it and there is no partnership agreement. But it is an intrinsic partnership: other NGOs cannot succeed unless STIR has prepared the soil, but STIR depends on other NGOs to plant the appropriate seeds of success: these seeds might be literacy or numeracy programmes, use of data in schools, improving school leadership and management.

Explicit partnerships are much harder to form, much harder to sustain but they can be much more productive. In some cases, they may be the only way of solving a challenge. Some problems are so complex that no single agency can solve it. For instance, the problem of prisoners re-offending is huge: roughly two out of every three will re-offend (and be caught and sentenced) within two years of release from prison. There are several hundred charities working in this area, offering everything from needlework to drug addiction courses to help offenders find their feet in society again. But isolated initiatives do not work: the re-offending rate has remained constant for decades. This is not surprising, because offenders often have complex and chaotic lives: lack of skills, or even lack of literacy and numeracy; rejection by employers and often by family (if there is one); no housing; no savings; inability to access government support services; drug dependency and mental health problems. The only way to address such a complex challenge is through an integrated approach: a needlework project cannot by itself solve the re-offending challenge.

If addressing the needs of one person is hard, then addressing the needs of an entire town is far harder. Governments are not set up to address problems of people or place. They are set up as very old-fashioned functional organizations, where housing, health, education, employment and justice are all separate functions. But the needs of both people and places encompass all these functions all at once. Separate government functions do not talk to each other and they have different budgets and different goals. Government cannot even make partnerships work across their own departments. This co-ordination problem is local as well as national. Local police, schools, hospitals, social services and housing associations rarely work together coherently, despite the best efforts of local councils and mayors.

The result of uncoordinated effort is huge waste and unfilled promise: left-behind towns which were once prosperous but have been passed by the passage of time find it hard to recover. This problem of control and co-ordination has been addressed by many quangos (quasi-autonomous non-governmental organizations) with little effect. Into this space has stepped an innovative charity called Right to Succeed. It lacks power to force control and co-ordination. Instead, it has to build coalitions of the willing to make change happen. This is extreme partnership working and is a work in progress, as the box below illustrates.

The greater the challenge, the greater the need to work in partnership. If even governments struggle to address the big problems alone, then your NGO will struggle even more. You cannot, and should not, try to do it all: you have to work with or alongside others to achieve your mission.

THE CHALLENGE OF PARTNERSHIP WORKING*

Right to Succeed was set up to address the inequity facing children and young people who are born and raised in low-income communities. It realized that piecemeal solutions that are designed at a distance do not work: only an integrated approach can solve deep-seated problems in disadvantaged communities. It is hard to achieve good education and social mobility outcomes across a community that is affected by the impact of poverty and the effect this has on families and their children.

As a small charity ($10 million turnover in 2024/25), Right to Succeed could not deliver the solutions itself, but it could act as a catalyst and integrate all the efforts of other organizations working on the same issue in the same place. As one exasperated head teacher in Blackpool exclaimed: 'We already have 90-plus initiatives in town. It is chaos, no one is in control. We don't need more initiatives, we need more focus and control.' Right to Succeed solves this problem by bringing focus and control: it helps to integrate the different initiatives working on children and families' outcomes in ten communities in England.

This partnership working is tough. The first challenge is to build a committed alliance for change. Schools, public services and community organizations need to be willing partners in

---

*The author was chair and part of the founding team of Right to Succeed, led by Graeme Duncan.

change: no one can tell them what to do. By joining the alliance for change, everyone has to give something up: schools give up some of their freedom of action; funders have to sign up to a programme which is not 'theirs' and delivery partners can no longer have the freedom to deliver what they want, when they want.

To build this alliance, Right to Succeed has to evaluate whether the conditions are right for success. There is no point in investing to fail. It will then design a programme of action which all the stakeholders can commit to: the programme has to be customized to the needs of each community. Typically, building the alliance for change will take six to 12 months from the initial discussion to agreeing the formal programme of action. Getting to that point involves endless discussions and debates. It is hard work. Working alone is far easier; working together is far more effective.

SCALE OR SCOPE?

The challenge of scale is obvious to most charities. Less obvious, but equally important, is the challenge of scope. Changing the world normally requires changing very complex systems. Even governments find it hard to change the complex system which we usually call 'Society'. A single NGO is unlikely to succeed where governments fail. You cannot change a complex system single-handed. You need partnerships to deal with the challenges of scope.

Many NGOs achieve success by scaling a single, simple idea. You may well believe that you hold the key to changing a system, but in practice you probably only hold one piece of the jigsaw of success. The jigsaw cannot be completed without you, so you are still key. However, one idea or one piece of the jigsaw does not present a complete picture. You have to find the other pieces of the jigsaw of success. Often, that means working with partners who can deliver the other pieces of the jigsaw. We have already seen how STIR Education recognizes this explicitly: it simply prepares the ground to allow other NGOs and government agencies to deliver their programmes successfully.

WHAT IS YOUR IMPACT?

We presented the schools minister with an offer we thought he could not refuse: 'Tell us what impact/change you want to make on the schools' system and we will deliver it. You pay us nothing until we have delivered the impact. All you have to do is to say what you want and how much you will pay us for achieving the impact.'

The minister conferred with his officials for a moment and then said: 'Well, of course, what we really want to see is an improvement in basic literacy and numeracy.' An aide then whispered in his ear. 'And of course,' the minister continued, 'we need to see progress in science and technology, the skills of the future.' He paused and then added, 'Foreign languages are also vital for a trading nation and we cannot ignore the humanities: history, geography, literature and things like that.'

By now the minister was in full flow, his officials were scribbling furiously in their notebooks: 'But it should not be all about exams. We need to look after the whole child. Sports and clubs like music, drama and poetry matter. And we need to help children build resilience and learn how to cope with the world, from social media to sex education and financial literacy. Then there are those essential employability skills, like teamwork, creativity and problem solving, which they must master. And we need to make sure that disadvantaged children and children with special needs are looked after; we need to help schools more in areas of economic deprivation. And at the other end, we need to make sure gifted and talented children achieve their full potential...'

'But what do you want to focus on?' we asked.

'All of it, of course!' he replied.

It is easy to mock foolish politicians and civil servants who do not even know what they want to achieve but if you had to decide what change to make in education, where would you focus? Systemic change is difficult because systems are complex.

When you want to achieve 20 goals at the same time, you will achieve none of them very well. To have impact, you need to be clear about where and how you will focus. And you need to be clear how that impact will work across the whole system, in conjunction with other initiatives. Your impact does not live in isolation: it is one piece of a constantly changing jigsaw puzzle.

Fitting your piece of the jigsaw into the rest of the picture is exceptionally hard work. You have to keep on shaping your idea to fit local conditions, which are constantly changing anyway. You are dealing with a jigsaw which has a mind of its own and keeps on shifting shape; the partners you work with keep on shifting as well and so you have to keep on changing just to keep up. In practice, this feels like a never-ending round of partner discussions about goals, scope, focus, budgets, reporting and co-ordination. It is draining and distracting work, although vital. But there is another way of dealing with this complexity: extend the scope of what you do to offer something closer to a turnkey solution. If you own the jigsaw puzzle, it is much easier to control what happens.

The *Big Issue* illustrates the challenge of scale versus scope and has been hugely successful. Having scaled up to a circulation of 57,000 copies in the UK in 2023, it has replicated into nine other countries. It provides a way for the homeless to earn money and become more self-reliant but it is clearly not a solution to homelessness. The Greater London Authority reports that rough sleeping more than doubled in London in ten years to 2024.* Part of this results from unintended consequences: selling the *Big Issue* enables migrants to the UK to

---

*Rough sleeping in London (CHAIN reports). Published by: Greater London Authority. Last updated: 10 May 2024. https://www.data.gov.uk/dataset/fe580c43-1754-4c15-baa0-1936a7f484d8/rough-sleeping-in-london-chain-reports

claim that they are self-employed, which then allows them to access UK benefits and housing programmes. The *Big Issue* undermines its own success. Like many charities, the *Big Issue* may not solve the problem, but it can help stop it getting worse.

In contrast to rising rough sleeping in London, in Helsinki rough sleepers have more or less disappeared. This is just as well, given winter temperatures can fall as low as -20 centigrade, which would be a death sentence for a homeless person. Broader homelessness has also declined across Finland from over 18,000 in 1987 to under 4,000 in 2021.* In 2007, the Finnish government decided to tackle homelessness with a comprehensive approach called 'Housing First'. They decided to give every homeless person an unconditional offer of a permanent home.

The ex-homeless can keep their home as long as they are interacting with social workers or no longer need support. In other words, the home is not the solution: it is the gateway to the solution. Once the homeless have a stable place to live, they can access the support to deal with the many complex problems they may have: mental health, lack of skills, substance dependency, lack of a job, lack of a mailing address and lack of support from family or friends. None of these problems can be addressed while they are still rough sleeping.

The challenge of homelessness illustrates the importance of scope not just scale. The *Big Issue* does great work for many people, but it can never solve the problem of homelessness by itself. It has to be part of a comprehensive suite of solutions which work for each homeless person. This is the same as most problems: re-offending, educational under-achievement, climate change cannot be solved by a single magic bullet. They all are problems with wide scope which need a wide range of complementary solutions.

Delivering an integrated solution requires extensive capability as well as capacity: you need a range of skills and interventions to fix a

---

*https://world-habitat.org/news/our-blog/helsinki-is-still-leading the-way-in-ending -homelessness-but-how-are-they-doing-it-2/

systemic problem. This is how Grameen works. As we have already seen, it is not simply a bank which makes loans. It works with groups of clients to help them collectively change their lives through better farming practices, better education and better health choices. Doing that at scale requires huge resources: Grameen Bank has over 20,000 employees.

Clearly, most NGOs do not have the capability or capacity to deliver an integrated solution in the way that the Finnish government addresses homelessness. While governments can throw money at a problem, you have to throw creativity at it. The reality is that your idea can only solve part of the problem. If you want to solve the whole problem, you will need help from other partners. In some cases, you may choose to focus on your own specialist intervention and hope that other NGOs and governments fix the rest of the problem. In effect, this approach is called hoping to get lucky. But hope is not a method and luck is not a strategy. If you want to ensure success, you need to have an active partner strategy to deliver the scope you need.

Some of the most original and effective partnerships can come with, and from, the private sector. Two examples will make the point (see box below):

PARTNERSHIPS TO ACHIEVE IMPACT THROUGH SCOPE

1. *Loop.*[*] Tom Szaky saw the huge waste in packaging. As CEO of a waste management firm, TerraCycle, he was well placed to do something about it. He set out to become the 'twenty-first century milkman' who would produce packaging that could be reused multiple times before being recycled. Loop packaging uses patented technology to make the circular economy a reality:

---

[*]*Revolution in a Bottle: How TerraCycle Is Eliminating the Idea of Waste* – 26 March 2013. By Tom Szaky with updates from TerraCycle annual reports and website: https://www.terracycle.com/en-US/

minimum waste through maximum recycling. But the circular economy only works if the traditional supply chain changes. Supply chains are normally one way, from producer to consumer. The circular economy requires a circular supply chain instead of a one-way supply chain, so Loop collaborates with 20 major partners such as P&G, Unilever, Coca-Cola and Nestlé. These huge firms are traditionally seen as environmental criminals with their enormous packaging waste and they are keen to improve their practices. Loop only succeeds if the whole system changes and that can only happen through partnerships.

2. *Cola Life.* [*] Jane and Simon Berry saw that Coca-Cola was able to distribute everywhere, even in the most challenging and remote communities in Zambia. At the time the leading cause of death for under-fives in these communities was diarrhoea. If they could distribute a simple kit, it would save many lives. Jane and Simon could not do that alone so they found partners to help them. They partnered with Janssen Pharmaceuticals to develop and design suitable kit which would fit in between the bottle necks in crates of Coca-Cola; they got the support of the Coca-Cola Corporation to work out how to achieve distribution; they also received training and support from Johnson & Johnson. Eventually, funding started to flow from the UK government's aid agency (DfID). Other partners helped them with monitoring and evaluation. On the ground, they partnered with Zambia's leading retailer, Shoprite, and many micro-retailers. The result is that diarrhoea treatment rates rose from 1 to 46 per cent in the target communities, partly because they were able to reduce the average distance travelled by caregivers buying the medicine from 7.3km to 4.2km.

Cola Life has had to invest a huge amount of effort into building partnerships, but the result is a system which requires little manpower: Cola Life had a grand total of three staff. By 2024

[*]https://www.colalife.org/

they had achieved their goals by embedding the distribution of diarrhoea treatment into government and the private sector, and Jane and Simon Berry then retired and closed Cola Life. This leaves a great opportunity for a social entrepreneur to replicate the success of Cola Life into other countries. As ever, you do not need to be creative to develop a great idea, you simply need to be observant and have the courage to take up an idea when it presents itself to you.

MONITORING AND EVALUATION (M&E)

If you have an idea to change the world, at some point you will want to know if you are succeeding. This can be elusive. If you work in the private sector, it is relatively easy to know if you are succeeding: your pay goes up, the profits and market share of your firm increase. For mission-driven organizations, success is much harder to measure. For instance, if you want to improve education, how do you know that your work has succeeded? Perhaps you can show that literacy has improved in the schools you serve, but has it improved faster than in other schools, what else has happened in your schools that might have improved literacy and has improved literacy come at the cost of taking focus away from other subjects and other needs of students?

If you work in an animal welfare charity, what does success look like? Is it the number of animals treated, which leads to treating simple conditions and ignoring difficult ones? Is success in the power of advocacy and getting animal welfare legislation passed? And how do you make decisions and decide priorities? In one animal welfare charity, the vets believed it is better to put an animal down than prolong its suffering. Other animal lovers believed that every life is sacrosanct, even if that means giving chemotherapy to a one-legged chicken. Between these extremes, there is a huge amount of contestable grey space where it is not obvious what the right decision might be, where to put resources and what success looks like.

Not knowing what success looks like means that decision making and resource allocation become emotional and political decisions, not rational decisions. It also means that you cannot have effective M&E because you do not know what you are meant to be monitoring and evaluating. Saying that you monitor 'animal welfare' is useless: it does not help you make decisions or allocate resources. The starting point for effective M&E is total clarity about what success looks like.

M&E can help you succeed in two different ways with two different constituencies, which require two different approaches:

1. *Proof of concept*: prove to funders, partners and stakeholders that they should continue to support you. This is known as summative assessment. The main focus is on finding out if you are succeeding, not how you are succeeding or what you might improve. It's a bit like passing or failing an exam at school.

2. *Programme improvement*: provide you with information about how and where your programme is working, and how you can improve it and use your limited resources better. This is known as formative assessment: typically, it is management information, which is a leading indicator of whether you are going to succeed in the summative assessment.

In practice, you will need both summative assessment (for proof of concept to key stakeholders) and formative assessment (to help management improve performance). These assessments can be both formal and informal. Formal assessments are structured evaluations, which might be carried out by a university or other independent body on your behalf. Informal assessments may involve personal visits to your programme or ad hoc surveys and reviews which you initiate. These differences are summarized in the diagram below. In practice, you will probably need to manage all four types of assessment, so we will cover each in turn.

Types of Monitoring and Evaluation

	Informal	Formal
Formative: *what can we learn?*	Management site visits Ad hoc surveys and reviews	Test markets Market research Tracking studies
Summative: *what can we prove?*	Site visits by funders and other stakeholders Informal reviews and presentations	Randomized Control Trials Paired comparisons Independent evaluations

As Sherlock Holmes observed in the case of the dog that didn't bark, it is always worth noting what is not there. There is a complete absence of charities' favourite form of evaluation, which is a summative self-evaluation. Many charities lack the time, resource or capability to do a rigorous and independent summative analysis of their performance. Instead, they create their own metrics, which they monitor themselves. This will convince the charity that they are doing a great job, but it will convince no one else: both the metrics and the method will lack credibility. Few people would trust a referee who is actually playing for one side. In practice, this is what many charities do: they play, and they try to be their own referee. Then they are indignant when no one believes their results.

In many cases the metrics are simply not credible. For instance, one charity claims to be doing great work at helping children who are at risk of being excluded from school for poor behaviour. They produce copious evidence of the number of children they have worked with; they have surveys which they have administered showing that the students who filled in the survey like the programme. And then they have tear-jerking video testimonials from some teachers and students. Unfortunately, this proves absolutely nothing:

- The number of children worked with is meaningless: how many were really at risk of exclusion or not? What was the impact of working with them? Did those who received the intervention do better than children who received no intervention at all?
- The survey data is meaningless. Children who liked the programme are more likely to respond to the survey than those who hated it. The survey does not tell us how much at risk these children were, or whether they went on to be excluded. Critically, there is no comparison with children who did not receive the programme or an alternative programme: the survey tells us nothing about whether the programme made a difference or not.
- Tear-jerking videos are great fundraisers, especially at big corporate fundraising dinners when everyone is slightly drunk. But finding a few people to say something nice about your programme proves nothing about its efficacy relative to other possible programmes, or to having no programme at all: anecdotes are not evidence.

Credibility is in the eye of the beholder. You may passionately believe that you have highly credible performance metrics but that is irrelevant if the key decision makers think that it is not credible. This was the case when we focused on reducing re-offending. We believed that we had a rock-solid indicator of our programme: people who went through the programme would either go on to re-offend or not. We measured that and believed it was 100 per cent credible, only to find that the government (our key funder) did not believe it was credible at all (see case study below).

REDUCING RE-OFFENDING… OR NOT?

Start Up* developed a great programme to help offenders set up their own, legitimate businesses on release from prison. Of the first 500 businesses set up by the ex-offenders, only four individuals got recalled to prison. Two of these were not for crimes, but for failing to follow their parole conditions correctly. In any event, it appeared that less than 1 per cent of Start Up clients went on to re-offend. The national average re-offending rate is 66 per cent within two years.

We approached government for funding to take the programme national: we estimated that about 9,000 offenders a year could benefit from our programme. Potentially, we could remove 6,000 re-offenders from the system every year: this would save nearly £200 million annually at a cost to government of just £16 million annually.

The government refused to fund the project because they said our 99 per cent success rate failed to reduce re-offending.

WTF???

Government argued that we were cherry-picking offenders. The offenders who came on to our programme would not have re-offended anyway. Simply by signing up to our programme, they showed that they were already prepared to go straight, so we added no value at all. If we wanted to prove our programme, we would have to put a randomly selected group of prisoners through the programme and compare it to a control group of prisoners who were not on the programme.

This put Start Up in an impossible position. We could not disprove the government's assertion that our clients were not going to re-offend anyway, even though the government had precisely zero evidence for their claim. And their proposal for a randomized

*Given government intransigence and incompetence, Start Up has pivoted away from its original mission. This is another great opportunity for a social entrepreneur to pick the idea up and make it work with a more amenable government. The author was founding chair of Start Up.

control trial was nonsense. At most 10 per cent of prisoners are willing and able to start their own businesses: the trial would have involved working with 90 per cent of clients who were completely unsuitable.

We learned that it really does not matter how impressive your results are, if they are not believed by the decision makers who matter. You need to get them to agree the metrics and the method before you start your programme. Bake credibility into your results from the start.

To understand what works, we will briefly review the four main types of M&E outlined in the diagram above. To recap, they are:

1. Informal formative: what can we learn from our own internal reviews?
2. Formal and formative: what can we learn from external assessments, test markets and tracking data?
3. Informal summative: what can we prove through informal work with external stakeholders?
4. Formal summative: what can we prove through independent evaluations which are agreed to be credible by our key stakeholders?

We will explore each of these four approaches in more detail below:

1. Informal formative assessment

This is all about management learning how to do things better and cheaper. Doing things better is clearly important because that drives impact. Doing things cheaper is vital because that helps drive scale. The path to growth is built on stripping your programme down to its core: you have to find your magic sauce where you uniquely can make a difference.

The easiest way to do a formative assessment is by walking around. Just get out there and see what is happening on the ground. You should quickly see what is and what is not working but there are two problems with this approach:

- You may not be objective enough to see what really matters
- Your staff may not be as keen on assessment as you are.

The chances are that you are too close to the operations to see them clearly and objectively. Often an outsider, or perhaps one of your board members, will see things differently. This can be deeply irritating and helpful at the same time. For instance, when I was building a business in Japan, a bigwig came from Germany to do a bit of seagull management: fly by and drop s**t. After two days of inspecting our work (and in advance of his holiday in Japan), I asked him what he had learned. The grand total of his wisdom was this: 'They don't speak English!'. He was right: no one had been able to talk to him in English. From this very trite and basic observation came some very important changes. Although we were a global organization, we decided to make our Japan business more Japanese: ensure that at least 98 per cent of staff and management were Japanese so that we could respond better to local needs. Sometimes, the biggest insights are the simplest. As the novelist George Orwell once wrote: 'Seeing what is in front of your nose needs a constant struggle.'* Find someone to help you see the obvious.

Even if you are keen on organizational learning, your staff may be less keen. Learning implies that you want to improve, which in turn requires change. Staff often fear change. At worst, they fear they may lose their jobs. At best, they may have to change how they work, which means learning new skills and having new performance goals. Many staff prefer to stick with existing skills and goals where they know they can succeed.

In practice, change is easiest under two conditions: rapid growth or rapid cutbacks. During rapid growth, everyone can see that change

---

*'In Front of One's Nose' in *Tribune*, 22 March 1946, George Orwell.

is good because it leads to more opportunities. They will be keen to learn and grow with the organization. We saw how STIR Education went through four iterations of its business model in seven years. Such rapid change was made far easier by the rapid growth which happened at the same time. It was relatively easy to foster a learning organization.

Rapid cutbacks are painful, but relatively easy. Staff are normally ready to adapt and change in order to avoid being part of the cutbacks: survival is a powerful motivator.

The hardest time to encourage learning and change is during steady state operations. During steady state, there is no obvious benefit to learning or changing. Most staff will be keen to protect what they have rather than try risky new ideas which may or may not work. In practice, you have to create a culture of learning. This means that learning has to be safe: mistakes should not be hidden or criticized, but valued for what can be learned from them. Learning needs to be how things are done, as with *Sesame Street* (*see* also p. 47 and the box below).

2. Formal and formative assessment

Formal assessment for learning can cover everything from test markets and pilots to tracking studies and market research. Where informal assessment can be anecdotal, formal assessment is rigorous and data driven. Again, the point of formative assessment is to learn and to improve; it is not to prove a point to stakeholders and decision makers.

The challenge is that even formative assessments tend to be gamed, for the best possible reasons. Everyone involved wants to show a success, not a failure. The best staff may land up working on the test; they will be working with the best partners and clients; extra management time and effort will focus on the test. One way or another, the test will be a success, but it will not be replicable or scalable.

Gaming of tests is most likely where tests are unusual. If you have a culture of testing everything, it becomes impossible to game every test. 'Test everything' is how *Sesame Street* works and it leads to a culture of deep learning.

SESAME STREET: BAKING RESEARCH INTO EVERYTHING YOU DO

Joan Cooney, co-founder of *Sesame Street*, said that 'without research, there would be no *Sesame Street*'. Research has been baked into the children's television programme from before it even started. In 1967, prior to the launch of the programme, the makers consulted widely with experts in education, child development, media and psychologists. Since launching, they have tested anything and everything to make sure it works. They constantly make mid-course adjustments when they find something is not working well. For instance, in a programme which focused on health, one character said, 'Eat your broccoli.' Research showed children did not like this message, so they changed the line to 'eat your colours', which got a positive response. Similarly, when the Mexican version of *Sesame Street* started in 1972, it had a crocodile character. Research showed that children were afraid of the crocodile, so the crocodile was promptly replaced by a Mexican version of Big Bird.

Sesame Street uses formative research to help make tough decisions on tough issues. For instance, they decided to tackle the topic of parental divorce. In 1992 they produced an episode called 'Snuffy's parents get a divorce.'* It bombed because it showed the parents arguing and then divorcing. They pulled the episode completely after testing it and started all over again: this time they only showed how everyone coped in the aftermath of a divorce.

Sesame Street regards every new season and every new country as an experiment. As with all experiments, they constantly test, learn and adapt. Their mantra is 'inform, improve, measure and repeat.'† During the season the focus is on formative assessment so that they can improve by making mid-course adjustments. At

*fromthegrapevine.com/arts/sesame-street-50-anniversary-science-research-study
†Cooney in Fisch & Truglio, p. xi

> the end of the season they focus on summative assessment to see if they have made the intended impact with the children they target.
>
> If you want to make an impact, you have to do the research.

Formative research is not about trying to prove a point, it is about insight to help you learn and adapt fast. That means you do not need academic levels of proof, or evidence which will stand up in a court of law: you need light touch research. Find the minimum required to generate the insight you require. With formative research, lots of small tests allow you to break things, change things and improve things at speed.

3. Informal summative assessment

It is normal to think that summative assessment is formal, like exams or selection interviews. In practice, many summative assessments are made quite informally. Most large organizations have sophisticated HR systems which provide summative assessments of staff: these inform bonus and promotion decisions. The value of these became clear when I ran a promotions commission for a global consulting group. We were faced with 60 promotion packs, all of which came through the formal process and which showed that each candidate was quite exceptional. Unfortunately, we only had 30 promotions to give away. Quickly, the conversation turned to who knew each candidate and what they were really like. In practice, we knew that some of the promotion packs were works of fiction. Many of the judgements were made not on the formal summative assessments (promotion packs) but on the informal summative assessments (what we had observed with our own eyes and ears).

Informal summative assessments can be powerful, cruel and dangerous:

- *Powerful:* they are powerful because the informal view often colours reaction to the formal assessment. We are all prone to confirmation bias: if the formal assessment confirms our informal assessment, we believe it. If the formal assessment

differs from our informal view, we are much more likely to
challenge the credibility of the formal review.

- *Cruel:* informal summative assessments are cruel because
  they are often made in private, behind closed doors: we have
  no idea who is saying what about us. We may have no idea that
  the conversation is even happening, so we cannot influence
  it. For instance, I took a group of national policy makers to
  Blackpool to see what was being done to improve education
  there. We saw schools, met officials and inspected initiatives.
  On the train back to London I asked the senior policy maker
  what he made of it all. He simply asked: 'Who's in control?'
  With that one question he successfully challenged everything
  that was happening there. There were simply too many
  competing initiatives which were overwhelming the local
  schools and causing more problems than they solved. That
  short conversation led to some very difficult conversations
  with organizations which thought they were doing a great
  job, but were just confusing things. It was a cruel, powerful
  and necessary judgement made in private: that is the power
  of informal summative assessments.
- *Dangerous:* they are dangerous because informal assessments
  often do not follow the formal metrics or methods. They
  might look at a problem from a completely different angle.
  Several initiatives working in Blackpool were doing a good
  job in their own right, but simply did not fit the bigger
  picture: the formal judgement said they were doing a good
  job, the informal judgement said that they caused confusion.

It may seem that you are powerless to influence informal summative
judgements but this is not true. There are two ways you can influence
these assessments.

First, you can and should have a clear narrative about what you are
doing. This should be a very simple narrative that a funder can explain
to their board, or that an official can explain to any big bosses who
ask. Simplicity is vital. No one will remember your carefully crafted

PowerPoint presentation or the long Word document you drafted. They will not even remember three bullet points, because you are just one of a hundred other things they need to worry about, like buying the pet food. If they forget your three bullet points, that will not harm them; if they forget the pet food, they will have a pet that will remind them vigorously. Although your mission is very important to you, it is less important than pet food to others so keep it simple and make it memorable.

For instance, when we started STIR Education in 2011, we had a slightly complicated story about how we would help teachers re-discover their intrinsic motivation and that would lead to better educational outcomes. Because this was a new idea, it took quite some explaining. We had to simplify the matters: we showed that we were on a five-year learning journey to figure out what was really going to work. This was 'being humble to be ambitious': the humility came from recognizing that lasting system change requires deep learning and innovation. The ambition came from wanting lasting system change. This changed the narrative with our funders from 'what have you achieved?' to 'what have you learned?'. If we had focused on achievement in the early years, we would have learned nothing. By focusing on learning, we were able to achieve far more. Influencing the narrative is vital to your survival: make sure all your stakeholders share a simple narrative which helps you.

SELL YOUR NARRATIVE

For-profit and not-for-profit sectors have much to learn from each other. The power of narrative first became clear when I was running a business in Japan. When I arrived, I found it was losing money fast, had lost all its clients and had lots of bills to pay. I knew what the informal summative judgement would look like at global HQ: Japan is losing money, so close it. My career was starting to career towards a messy finale.

I created an alternative narrative, framed as a choice between three options:

- Close the business and be excluded from the Japan market for a generation or more (totally unacceptable);
- Buy a Japanese business and build that up (very expensive, very risky and very hard to do);
- Invest in growing the existing Japan business organically for three years on the path to profitability (low cost, low risk).

Inevitably, everyone chose option three, which gave me licence to lose money ('invest in organic growth') for three years. HQ was not keen on making losses but was keen on making smart investments, so I simply converted the idea of losses into investments. They had a narrative which pleased them and allowed me to lose money.

Selling this narrative, and selling your narrative, takes a huge amount of time and effort. The narrative never emerges fully formed on day one. You have to keep on talking, keep on refining your message and keep on repeating your message. Don't assume anyone has got your message until you hear them telling your message back to you.

The second way you can influence the informal judgement of your stakeholders is to bring them on a field visit, because seeing is believing. There is an inevitable risk with this: they may see things you do not want them to see and they may form views you do not want them to have. Much of this comes down to how you see your funders and other key players. If you have a traditional funder/grantee or vendor/buyer relationship, then you will want to keep your funders at arm's length. The alternative is to see them as partners in helping you craft and deliver your mission. Building partnerships is sufficiently important to merit its own chapter. At this stage, it is enough to note that you have more chance of creating a positive informal narrative if you are close to your key funders than if you have a more formal relationship with them.

The big message is simple: control your narrative or someone else will. Invariably, your narrative will be more positive and productive than a narrative which someone else creates for you.

4. *Formal summative assessments*

Formal summative assessments are like exams where you show how well you can perform. Unlike exams, you will find that each examiner or funder has a different question which they want you to answer and they want you to answer it in a different way. This can become very burdensome very fast. For instance, you may have a programme to improve literacy. It is relatively easy to test literacy levels, so that should make a formative assessment simple to design and execute. But then you find that different funders have quite different needs:

- Show progress over one, two or three years, or show how many students achieve a certain level
- Focus on urban or rural schools
- Focus on gifted and talented children or children with special educational needs
- Focus on different age groups or geographies
- Focus on the whole cohort and measure attrition, or only measure progress of those who complete the programme
- Measure the effect on children directly involved in the programme or measure the effect across the whole school.

These are all potentially big decisions because what you measure is what you get. To make matters worse, random events can scupper your best-laid evaluation plans. Many NGOs found that all their evaluation programmes became useless when the Covid-19 pandemic struck: beneficiaries and delivery staff simply became unavailable and programmes stopped.

Measuring the right thing the right way matters. What you measure shapes your programme: where you will focus and what you will do. Finding the right thing to measure is hard enough, finding the right way is even harder.

The gold standard for formal summative assessments are RCTs: randomized control trials. This is a methodology borrowed from medicine, where RCTs are used to test the efficacy of new drugs and different treatments. The trial compares one group which received the treatment and another which did not receive it. In theory, this approach is very sound. In practice, it is often very challenging for at least six reasons:

1. Strategic
2. Operational
3. Technical
4. Ethical
5. Financial
6. Practical.

Strategic. Different funders and partners want you to measure different things because they want to achieve different things. Your decision about what to measure is a big strategic decision because that will focus your resources and efforts for the period of the trial. You cannot avoid the decision to focus. If you chose to measure everything, you will probably achieve nothing. At this point you may find that the tail is wagging the dog: your M&E plan is dictating your strategy. Some funders are sufficiently enamoured with RCTs that they find themselves backing medical interventions, simply because those are the ones where RCTs work the best: cause and effect is clear in medical interventions, but muddy in complex social systems where a single effect has many causes. RCTs can force you to ignore big social challenges.

Operational. (1) The minor operational problem is that summative assessments take a huge amount of effort to run. For example, one donor got very upset that we could not track school attendance of girls to the level of accuracy they expected. Tracking was impossible because we were working in the bad lands of Northern Kenya: severe drought and violent incursions from Somalia meant that whole communities were on the move, simply to survive. Keeping accurate school rolls, in a semi-literate part of the world, was not a survival priority for them.

Operational. (2) A summative assessment is, inevitably, a lagging indicator of performance. This can make it useless. One RCT was run on a programme to build resilience in children. To measure this properly, the funders wanted to measure the effects on both resilience and academic performance over five years, with time added on for setting up and for reading results at the end. By the time the positive results came out, the charity which ran the programme had more or less collapsed financially and had completely changed its product offering anyway. In practice, nothing stays the same over five years or more: trials which last too long may look good academically but have no practical value.

Technical. Getting the design of an RCT, or any other method, right is both hard and important. Details matter. You will have to live with the trial potentially for years: you do not want to find out at the end of a three-year programme that the results have been compromised by a faulty design. For instance, we wanted to look at the impact on children's learning if teachers rediscovered their intrinsic motivation. After two years, we found that the researchers were focusing on the results for the whole school, not just on the 20 per cent of teachers who received the intervention. That made it more or less impossible to assess the effect on individual teachers and learners. The trial was not worthless, but it was compromised.

Ethical. A proper RCT requires that you have two groups: one which receives the treatment and one which does not. To avoid selection bias, you have to recruit twice as many people as you need: for each two people you recruit, one will randomly be assigned to the treatment group and one will not receive the treatment. If you have an intervention which works, and you have people who have signed up to the treatment, it is ethically problematic to then deny the treatment to those people.

Financial. To have much chance of achieving a statistically significant difference between the two groups, you normally need to have a large group of at least 1,000 participants. This is the sort of thing which governments and pharmaceutical companies, who have deep pockets, can organize relatively easily. Organizing this sort of a trial is far beyond the financial means or capabilities of most NGOs. Occasionally, it is just impossible. We wanted to test an intervention which improved the leadership of a whole school: results would be based on whole school performance. That meant we would have to recruit up to 2,000 schools: 1,000 to receive the treatment and 1,000 not to receive the treatment. Recruiting even one school takes huge time and effort: recruiting 2,000 was impossible. In the end, we had to work with 20 schools: to achieve a statistically significant improvement with just 20 schools required a scale of impact which has never been achieved, and probably never will be achieved. The RCT had failure baked in from the start.

Practical. The whole point of a formal summative assessment is to prove that your intervention works to people who make decisions. Before you start, you have to ask: what am I proving and who am I proving it to? It does not matter if you believe in the trial, the trial has to be credible with the people you are trying to prove something to. You must involve these stakeholders and get their explicit support for the trial, and link it to an explicit decision: if we prove this, then will you fund that? Summative assessments are not about making you feel good, they are about getting decisions made in your favour.

Even if you can overcome all of these problems, you will find that summative assessments are not about learning or improving how you do things. They are about passing an exam. This is a burden which donors have a right to impose on you. Your donors need to know that their money is having the effect they desire. In the absence of reliable performance data, funders would be investing blind. Your challenge is to work with your donors to make sure you have an assessment which works. That means you need a real partnership discussion with your donors about how to make the assessment work. The questions you need to answer jointly include:

- What is the purpose of the assessment? What decision will the donor make, and how and when, based on the assessment?
- What does success look like? This is the big question, because the answer will drive your strategy: what you measure is what you get. Different donors have different versions of success: ideally, you should bring them together to agree a common vision.

- Who pays? The costs of assessment are not just the costs of hiring the market researchers, university or consultants to run the assessment. Someone also has to pay for your costs of running the assessment. If the donors really want the assessment, they should pay for it.
- What is the methodology? This needs to be practical from your perspective and credible from the donor's perspective. You will want a simple, light touch method; the donor will probably want a gold-plated assessment. Find the middle ground.
- Who will design and deliver the assessment? The right people will understand the brief, be adaptable and make sure they get the technical details right for you. The wrong people may be prestigious and brilliant, but if they force you into their rigid way of doing things, it will not be a good experience.
- How will we know if we are on track? You cannot wait until the end to hear results. You need some way of knowing how things are progressing, so that you can ditch the assessment or develop an alternative. You also need to know who assesses the assessors and what you will do in the event of disagreements and problems.

Embedding M&E in your organization
The United Nations Development Programme recommends spending 3–5 per cent of your budget on M&E.* Other large NGOs, such as Oxfam and Save the Children, target similar budgets. That works if you are a very large NGO with deep pockets. It becomes more or less impossible for smaller charities. The cost of an RCT is largely fixed: you need a minimum scale to make an RCT work. A large organization can afford to spend $100,000 to $500,000 on assessment. That is

*https://www.evalcommunity.com/donors-and-nonprofit/budget-allocation-for-monitoring-and -evaluation-me/

simply not possible for a small organization that is probably struggling to make ends meet. This is unhealthy because good M&E is central to any organization's ability to learn, innovate, grow and make its case to funders.

Charities often feel guilty about spending any money which is not directly executing programmes, so they underinvest in building organizational capacity. This means that not only M&E is underinvested, but so too are other vital functions like finance, IT, training and HR. This inability to invest properly in capacity building is aided and abetted by many funders who only want to invest in programmes, not in infrastructure or what they see as the dead weight of overhead expenses. They want the cake you bake, but are only prepared to pay for the ingredients: they assume that the cost of all the labour, the kitchen, the equipment, staff training and all other overheads miraculously pay for themselves.

By spending so little on M&E, most charities are not very good at it. They lack the in-house skills to know how to manage M&E. This puts them at the mercy of external contractors who design and deliver M&E for them. These partners may be universities, market research firms or consultants. Each one has its value and each one has its biases. Lacking in-house M&E skills makes it very hard to commission effective M&E.

IMPACT: SUMMARY

To have impact, you will need to scale the mission but not necessarily the organization. Success at scale requires a different formula from your startup success. Startups are fuelled by passion and enthusiasm. At scale, you need a stable and sustainable delivery machine.

Your growth journey is a learning journey. This requires patient and understanding funders. To be truly ambitious you have to be humble enough to learn and adapt.

You have five main routes to scale, which often overlap:

- Organic growth, which enables you to retain control but is probably unaffordable at scale.
- Mergers with other charities, but they are both rare and hard to achieve.
- Replicating your model (*Sesame Street*): local partnerships let you control what is core to your success while allowing for local variation.
- Build a movement (Teach for All) which is locally responsive and fast to grow. There will be variation around the world and tensions between the centre and the local operation. Control over local partners is hard to achieve.
- Build partnerships, especially with governments for delivery at scale. But governments can be unreliable partners and it is easy to lose control.

Impact requires not just scale, but scope. You hold only part of the solution to the jigsaw. You will need to work with other NGOs, governments or private sector to deliver a truly systemic solution.

M&E is vital to your success for both learning what works and proving you are succeeding. It is both formative and summative and informal and formal:

- Informal formative: internal reviews to learn and improve. 'Management by walking around'.
- Formal formative: formal test markets and pilots to discover what works, often internally run.
- Formal summative: traditional M&E to prove to funders and partners whether your programme works. This M&E will dictate your focus and priorities, it is important and dangerous. Pre-agree with funders the shape and purpose of this M&E.
- Informal summative: judgements made about you informally by third parties. Ensure you control the narrative about how your NGO is perceived.

3

People

Create and sustain the winning team

Any venture capitalist or investor will tell you that an idea is only as good as the people who stand behind it. An average idea from a great team will be made into a great idea by the team. A great idea from a mediocre team will become mediocre as the team struggles to overcome modest obstacles and waters down its ambition. This chapter covers two core people themes: the founder and the team. It will deal with the following challenges:

The founder:

1. *Have you got what it takes to change the world?*
2. *How to take the first steps on your journey to changing the world*
3. *How your role changes over time*
4. *Founder syndrome, and how you can avoid it.*

The team:

5. *How to recruit a strong startup team*
6. *How your team has to change as you grow*
7. *How to manage your team.*

1. HAVE YOU GOT WHAT IT TAKES TO CHANGE THE WORLD?

The good news is that you do not need to be superhuman to change the world. Anyone can change the world. In practice, social entrepreneurs have four characteristics:

- Passion for a particular cause
- Acceptance that they have to be the agents of change
- Basic skills and capability
- Naivety about the scale of the challenge they face.

PORTRAIT OF A SOCIAL ENTREPRENEUR: TOM RAVENSCROFT

Tom Ravenscroft founded the Skills Builder Partnership, which has changed the way people think about the curriculum in schools. Becoming a social entrepreneur had never been on his career plan. After leaving university he planned to go into consulting after completing the two-year Teach First programme.

Those plans went out of the window as he found himself drawn into the challenge of equipping children with the essential skills and employability skills they would need as adults. The challenge presented itself to him when he had to teach children for a qualification which made little sense. He did not find the mission, the mission found him. Tom found he was excited by it in a way that consulting did not excite. Each night, he had to set a 2 a.m. cut-off time for finishing work on developing his idea, which was a side hustle to his teaching job.

Like many social entrepreneurs Tom was both smart and naive about the risk and the challenge. He validated his idea from the safety of a secure job. His teaching qualification also gave him something to fall back on if it all went wrong. And with no dependents or mortgage, he could afford to take risks. In his words, 'I was very naive about the challenge. I did not really think through the opportunity cost of doing this, but in your twenties, you think

---

> you have all the time in the world. I am not sure I would do it now in my life, with a mortgage and dependents.' But in reality, it was not an entirely rational decision: 'I found I could not avoid doing it.' As with many social entrepreneurs, the call of the mission was irresistible.
>
> Tom recognizes the challenge of moving on. As with most social entrepreneurs, operational work does not excite him. If Skills Builder Partnership becomes a steady state operational job, he will move on. Most social entrepreneurs are also more excited about building the idea and the model rather than on the grind of execution. When the time comes, they find it very hard to move on from the success they have created.

Passion for a particular cause
Successful social entrepreneurs are evangelical about their cause. This really matters, because you need vast depths of resilience to overcome the many obstacles which you will face. If you are totally committed to your cause, you will find a way round any problem. In this respect, social entrepreneurs are like top sports stars, musicians and mountaineers who go through hell to achieve their goals. Looking back, most admit that they were obsessive: weekends disappear, birthdays and family events are constantly at risk or just get missed and exhaustion is normal.

Talking to social entrepreneurs, it is often hard to get them to shut up: they want everyone and anyone to know about their mission. They start to get tunnel vision – not much else matters to them, at least until they have built their NGO to a point of sustainability. Then they can let their team take some of the strain as they step back, marginally.

Only you know if you have the passion to go through with your idea. It is not enough to want to pursue your idea. The idea will eat away at you non-stop until eventually you realize you have no choice: you have to go through with it. Pursuing your dream becomes an existential crisis: you simply can't not do it.

Acceptance that they have to be the agents of change
Curiously, social entrepreneurs do not always set out to change the world directly themselves. They only take on the role of change agent when it is clear that no one else will. Muhammad Yunus was a professor at a university in Bangladesh and had no intention of setting up Grameen Bank. He repeatedly tried to get local banks to take up his idea. They demanded ever-tougher proofs of concept, which he delivered time and again. After seven years of being messed around, he finally realized that the banks had zero interest in serving the poor. The only way that his concept would get to scale would be if he set up a bank himself.

This is a typical reaction. Yunus was not ambitious for himself: he was content to remain a university professor, but he was very ambitious for his idea. As with many social entrepreneurs he was a curious mix of humility and ambition: be humble personally, but ambitious for your mission. His passion for alleviating poverty through micro finance trumped his desire to remain a university professor. He simply had to follow through on his idea. Time and again, entrepreneurs recall how they felt that they had no choice but to start their social enterprise.

As you think about your idea, you may also be tempted to ask other people to make your dreams come true for you. That is a recipe for years of frustration and disappointment, because no one will have the same level of passion for your idea as you do. To avoid wasting years of your life, be ready to move to action yourself sooner rather than later.

Basic skills and capability
You do not need to be a management genius to start up. Most CEOs of social enterprises are an MBA-free zone. This is probably a good thing. Following orthodox management practices would be a good way to kill your idea at birth. To survive, your idea will need skills which you can acquire at speed through experience, but which are very hard to learn from books or courses. These skills include:

- Creativity to adapt your idea in light of emerging experience, fresh information and new ideas.
- Flexibility and focus to work out how to make each dollar of income produce three dollars of value: you will become very creative at resource management.
- Networking ability, to attract supporters, donors, partners and team members.
- Strong work ethic and an ability to multi-task: you have to keep on top of multiple agendas at the same time.

You do not need formal training in financial skills, marketing, operations management, IT or HR. These skills are all vital and you deal with them by building a great team around you of volunteers, supporters and paid staff. Leadership is a team sport, so build the right skills around you.

SKILLS OR MONEY?

In the contest for survival, skills trumps money every time. With the right skills, a small amount of money can lead to huge returns. With poor skills, even a large amount of money will soon be frittered away. Your critical resources are not time and money, but time and skills. This lesson came home to me while supporting two startup social enterprises.

Enterprise A: STIR Education.
Sharath Jeevan decided to address the UN challenge of 300 million children in school but not learning. That is a huge challenge, for which he had no money. He took an initial £3,000 donation to scope out his idea. STIR Education is now turning over $3 million a year and is serving over 6 million children, and their teachers and government officials, in four countries. As with the mythical stories of the tech billionaires who all started out in a garage or their bedroom, the reality is that when you

---

have a great idea and a great person, you need very little money to ignite success.

Enterprise B: the one that got away

The enterprise started well. It had a £300,000 endowment; it had exclusive rights to a world-class intervention in schools which worked; it had a business plan drawn up by experts. It had a better starting product and more financial strength than STIR had at inception. What could possibly go wrong?

Twelve months later, the charity was on the brink of collapse. It had more or less exhausted its endowment and had generated no significant alternative sources of funding. The CEO was very clear that this was the fault of the staff who had let her down; advisors who had wasted her time; accountants who did not tell her what was happening, partners who were unsuitable and board members who were useless. Her initial passion for the idea had turned into fury with everyone connected to the charity.

Both charities started out with passionate leaders who believed in the cause; both had a great idea. The right leader will attract the right supporters, donors and team who can assure success. The successful entrepreneur is not a lone hero, despite what the ghostwritten autobiographies in airport bookshops would have you believe. Success is a team effort. You will never have all the skills you need to succeed yourself: build the skills you need in the team around you.

The successful startup lacked funds, the unsuccessful one was awash with them. The difference between the two was the ability of the CEO to build a strong team to deliver the vision.

Naivety about the scale of the challenge they face
It is questionable how many soldiers would want to go to war if they really knew what they faced. It is also questionable how many social entrepreneurs would start up if they really knew what they faced. As

one entrepreneur put it: 'Ignorance is bliss.' There will be plenty of people who offer you unhelpful advice about all the challenges and problems you face. Most successful entrepreneurs have remarkably deaf ears when it comes to hearing about problems; they spend their whole time looking for solutions. Denial can be dangerous if you ignore obvious pitfalls, but it is also very useful in helping you sustain belief in your ability to stay the course.

Fortunately, by the time you realize how tough it is, you will have already burned all your bridges. You will be fully committed. Do not dwell too much on the harsh reality which awaits: everyone else has been through it and you can survive it as well. As ever, the key to survival is to get help. You need help to complete tasks, and you also need personal support. It can be very lonely as a leader because you never have a truly open and honest conversation. Every conversation has an explicit or implicit agenda and that can be deeply enervating. You need friends and family with whom you can decompress; you may also need a coach or mentor with whom you can talk through some of the tougher professional challenges you face.

The other way to overcome the many obstacles you will face is to keep your goal firmly in mind. You will find that the tougher the challenges, the sweeter success becomes. After the event, you may well find it hard to believe what you have achieved. For instance, when Brett Wigdortz and I set up Teach First in 2002 we understood neither the scale of the challenge we faced, nor the scale of success it would become. Fifteen years after starting up, we attended the Teach First annual conference in Leeds. There were over 2,000 people there in a huge conference hall, complete with a corporate village and media. We wandered around in slight disbelief that this had all emerged from an initial cup of tea together. 'Have we really done this?' we asked ourselves. In truth, the answer was 'no': thousands of great people over many years had made it all possible. But it was a moment to savour success. When you are in the valley of despair, never doubt that you will reach the mountains of success.

PORTRAIT OF A SOCIAL ENTREPRENEUR: NICOLA SHARP-JEFFS*

Surviving Economic Abuse deals with the challenge that domestic abuse is often linked to economic abuse and economic control. This makes it very hard for the victim to escape the abusive relationship. You have to deal with economic abuse to deal with domestic abuse. Nicola Sharp-Jeffs saw the problem and found that no one was dealing with it. She then started a classic journey to social entrepreneurship:

- *Passion for a particular cause*
  'I talked to survivors (of economic abuse) who could have been me. It was very insidious.' Nicola started to write about the issue and campaign around it, hoping that others would initiate the change. The turning point came when she received a Winston Churchill Fellowship to travel and study, which allowed her to find out how other countries were starting to deal with economic abuse: both the problem and potential solutions came into sharp relief.
- *Acceptance that they have to be the agents of change*
  'It took me ten years to act on it. Once I saw what could be done it just took me over. Everything else became very dreary, very unfulfilling. I just couldn't not do it.' Slowly, Nicola realized that if she did not act, no one would act. She finally took the leap and set up the charity when she unexpectedly received a government grant. Her hand was forced: she had to step up or step out. Stepping out was never a serious proposition. It was a predictably messy transition. At one time she was 'juggling a job writing a paper, finishing my doctorate and starting the charity'.

*Original interview with the author. Nicola is founder of SEA and was CEO from 2017 to May 2024.

- *Basic skills and capability*
  Nicola had already built extensive experience working as a director at Missing People and at Refuge: she understood the sector. She also has great networking ability. This helped her raise the profile of the issue through an appearance on the BBC's *Woman's Hour* and through good access to civil servants who helped her with her initial grant applications.
- *Naivety about the scale of the challenge they face*
  'I knew it was risky. I was scared. But I did not know what was really involved. Blissful ignorance at the time. I have never been so exhausted.' But Nicola was quick to get help. She started alone in early 2018. By July she had her first team member and now there are 31 staff:* never doubt the ability of a few people to have a huge impact.

Surviving Economic Abuse works by making system change, which means few people can make a big difference. Nicola works with government to change policy; she has helped banks change their policies and systems so that they can help identify economic abuse and she is helping build capacity in other welfare organizations (as well as banks) so that they can identify and deal with economic abuse better. The next step is to set up a funded help line to give direct support to victims of domestic abuse. For a new and small organization, it is already transforming the way that economic abuse is recognized and dealt with.

No social entrepreneur is ever fully prepared for the challenges of a startup. Nor will you ever have all the skills needed to succeed. This is very good news. No leader gets ticks in all the boxes. If you have commitment, basic skills and an ability to build a good network of funders, staff and supporters, then you have the raw ingredients of

---

*Correct at the end of the 2022/23 financial year. https://register-of-charities.charitycommission.gov.uk/charity-details/?regId=1173256&subId=0

success. You will learn the other skills you need very fast and in real time. With the right support, you can overcome any challenge.

2. HOW TO TAKE THE FIRST STEPS ON YOUR JOURNEY TO CHANGING THE WORLD

Starting up is scary. A short adrenaline rush at the fun fair may be exciting, a three-year adrenaline rush of a startup is exhausting. So how do you make the leap into the unknown, from the comfort of a safe job and a regular salary? The simple message is 'look before you leap'.

Most social entrepreneurs spend a long time exploring the feasibility of their idea before they leap. They then experience a moment of truth where they are forced to make a decision. Here are a few examples from entrepreneurs featured in this book:

- Muhammad Yunus spent seven years doing proof of concepts of his idea while still working at university. By the time he decided to start Grameen Bank he had an idea which he knew would work. The catalyst for action was yet another refusal by the banks to adopt his idea.
- Nicola Sharp-Jeffs spent ten years working on economic abuse, including a Winston Churchill Fellowship to find out how the issue was being tackled elsewhere. She was pushed to starting up when the government made a grant: she had to set up a charity and bank account at speed to accept the money.
- Brett Wigdortz took leave of absence from McKinsey & Company to work on the startup of Teach First. In theory, that left him a route back if the idea did not work out. When the government, at the second attempt, approved the idea, he was irreversibly committed.
- Starting a bank took me two years of working on and adapting the idea while still a partner at Accenture. The moment of truth came when I approached a client to see if he would join my startup team. To my surprise, the CEO agreed. That was the point when I either had to pack in my idea or pack in my day job: there was an unsustainable conflict of interest.

- Sharath Jeevan worked on the idea for STIR Education while still the CEO of another charity, Teaching Leaders. As soon as the first funders came on board, he was committed: when you accept the money, you have to deliver the results.

All of this is smart risk management. During this transitional phase you will follow a simplified version of the IPM agenda which is reduced to:

- Idea
- People
- Money.

This transitional phase is essentially an extended feasibility study. In the corporate world, a feasibility study often asks if a project is viable. As a true social entrepreneur you will not be asking *if* your project is viable, but *how* it is viable. You will have to flex and adapt, but there is likely to be no question in your mind about whether you should chase your goal. Here is what the IPM agenda looks like in the transition phase:

Idea. This is the time to road test your idea and see if it has any chance of success. Invariably, you will find that you need to adapt it as you go along. The way you can develop your idea is by talking to lots of people. Don't worry about them stealing your idea: they are too busy, they do not have the same degree of passion and commitment as you and they can only see part of the picture you are building.

People. As you talk to people about your idea, you will also be building a coalition of the willing. People will naturally select themselves in or out. Those who suck air over their gums and tell you how difficult it is going to be, select themselves out. People who get excited and start working out solutions for you select themselves in. There is then some delicate choreography you need to manage: you need to get everyone sufficiently excited that they are all prepared to commit at the same time. Normally, no one wants to be first to jump, so you have to get everyone to jump together.

Money. You will probably start with nothing but you do not need anything, because all you are doing is talking with people: that cost is no more than the price of a cup of coffee. As the transition phase develops, you will want to build confidence among your supporters that progress is happening. You may want to build a simple website so that new and existing supporters can check you out. You should also be able to get in kind support from businesses who will lend you meeting rooms and host small conferences if you need that.

During this transition phase you need to find a few angel investors who can throw in seed corn funding, then you can work on finding substantial funding from larger investors. Typically, it is money which is the catalyzing event that forces the end of the transition: when you receive significant investment, you will have to start delivering outcomes in return and that is when you move from talking to doing: your transition promptly ends.

MANAGING THE TRANSITION: STARTING TEACH FIRST

Idea

When starting Teach First, we were inspired by Teach for America but we had to adapt the idea for the English market. The adaptations were significant:

- Name: we tried 'Teach for Britain' to play the patriotic card. When the name came up in focus groups, we had to pass the sick bag around. We had to find another name.
- Value proposition: we offered graduates the chance to work twice as hard for half the salary they could get elsewhere. Not good. And patriotism did not work. Eventually, we focused on leadership: Teach First was to be the gateway to leadership in any profession.
- Training: trainee teachers used to take two years to be trained. We had to find a way in which they could be trained in six weeks.

People
Teach First needed the support of a huge range of stakeholders:

- Government: to licence the programme and pay for the initial teacher training.
- Unions to make sure graduates would be accepted and that they should not be paid too much ('elitism') or too little ('teaching on the cheap').
- University training provider to deliver the initial six-week training programme: this required a university which was ready to be revolutionary in the sector.
- Businesses who had to endorse the programme as a viable and attractive path to leadership and as a potential path into their own business so that graduates could see that joining Teach First would open up career options, not close them down.

Money
Initially, Teach First relied on seed corn funding from a few businesses and foundations. We had to wait until the big money came from government. Once government started funding, we could raise the level of expectations with other funders and businesses who could see that they would be supporting a viable, sustainable and scalable operation.

As part of managing money in the early days we did what all startups do: we boot strapped and blagged our way to securing resources and making them stretch. We were shameless about using the hospitality of McKinsey & Company as a meeting place and startup office: it gave visitors the impression that we knew what we were doing.

3. How your role changes over time

If you move from a corporate role to starting up a social enterprise, you will make some interesting discoveries about working life:

- It is possible to turn right at the aircraft door without dying

- Taxis or Ubers are not the only form of transport in the city
- Flowers are not necessary and do not change themselves
- Tea and coffee does not make itself and crockery does not clean itself
- Cash flow is not a tedious finance accounting concept: it is the difference between being in business or going bust
- IT, HR, legal, finance and facilities management are not annoying corporate overheads: they are essential services which you are now going to have to deliver yourself.

All of this means that when you start out, you are likely to find yourself doing everything. That also means you will be working all hours at real cost to your family and social life. It is worth having conversations with your family about this before you plunge in: they will be bearing much of the domestic and emotional burden on your behalf.

Doing everything yourself is not sustainable, nor is it efficient or effective. You are unlikely to be an IT expert, accountant, lawyer and operations expert all rolled into one. There will be other people who can perform those tasks better and faster than you can. Even if you enjoy tinkering with websites and computers, that is not a good use of time for the founder. You need to focus your time where it has most effect, which is likely to be engaging stakeholders, building your team and overseeing delivery of your programme.

All founder CEOs find that their title never changes, but their role keeps on changing. You have to keep on promoting yourself in role. This process of continual promotion is about shedding lower-value activities and focusing on the few things where you make the most difference.

This promotion process is easy to start with. All founders are keen to shed administrative and technical work as soon as they can, but it becomes harder when you have to shed roles which you enjoy doing. Most founders want to be involved in the delivery of their service. This is natural: service delivery is the cutting edge of your mission. But staying involved at this level is dangerous for three reasons:

- It is probably not the best use of your time, and you are probably not the best person to deliver the service.
- You inadvertently make innovation harder: no one on the team will be willing to tell you that the model needs to be improved, or that you are not delivering it well.
- Not letting go shows that you do not trust other people can do the job as well as you. In practice they may be able to improve it. By showing you trust your team, you empower them and get the best out of them.

Letting go is really hard. You probably enjoy the work, you may doubt that others can do it as well as you and it is good displacement activity: it allows you to avoid doing the tough stuff which only you can do as CEO and founder.

If you ask yourself 'what can I stop doing?', you will find that there is very little you can stop doing. You will convince yourself that you are indispensable nearly everywhere so you need to ask a different question. The productive question is 'what is it that only the CEO can do?' This question produces quite a short but demanding list which might include:

- *External stakeholder engagement.* The CEO is the cheerleader-in-chief for the organization. You may have a fundraising team which does plenty of work in the background, but key funders and stakeholders invariably want to hear from the CEO.
- *Team formation and management.* You are only as good as the team you recruit and build. Build an outstanding top team and they will build the rest for you.
- *High-level governance.* This is about overall strategic direction and management of the board: you will need to reassure them on financial controls and management and compliance with the endless rules and regulations which entangle charities. This implies you need a very good chief financial officer and chief operating officer who can look after this for you, but you remain accountable for what they do.

Founders routinely find it hard to let go. Ultimately this is a sign that you do not trust other people to do the job as well as you can. If you cannot trust your team, either you have the wrong team or the team has the wrong leader. If you have the right team, you have to show you trust them by letting go and giving them responsibility. Inevitably, there is a question about how much you can let go at any point in time. There are two limits to this and these define what you can and cannot do:

- Funding: the less funding you have, the more you need to do yourself. The more funding you have, the more you can hire a team to do things for you. Scale is your friend, at least initially: it allows you to focus where you add most value.
- Time: if you are working too long, getting too tired and getting too stressed then you are doing too much. Do not try to be the lone hero who does it all: get your team to take the strain, subject to funding. Set yourself some limits in terms of working hours. When you exceed those limits that should be a clear message for you to delegate more.

RONALD REAGAN AND THE ART OF DOING LESS TO ACHIEVE MORE

Ronald Reagan was the 40th President of the United States. Comedians at the time liked to portray him as being both very lazy and very stupid. Where there is smoke, there is fire. He reputedly insisted on having a TV dinner in his pyjamas, watching the latest soaps, by 7 p.m. every night while he was president. That does not smack of overwork.

Although dumb and idle by reputation, Reagan was staggeringly successful: he had ambitious goals which he achieved. First, he wanted to deal with the 'Evil Empire' of the USSR. He did this by agreeing a breakthrough nuclear arms reduction treaty with them and then seeing the end of Communism itself as the Berlin

---

Wall came down in the year he left office, 1989. His second goal was to transform economics by deregulating and reducing taxes. This was so successful that it became known as Reaganomics in the USA and helped inspire Thatcherism in the UK.

So how can a dumb and idle leader be so successful?

Reagan did two things which all entrepreneurs can learn from. First, he built a talented team around him who did all the hard work of delivering his vision. That left the awkward question of what his role was, if everyone was delivering his vision for him. His role was to play to his greatest strength, which came from his days as a professional actor. He was the 'great communicator' who could appeal to both Congress and to the American people and persuade them to follow his vision. Selling the vision was not something his team could do, only the President could really sell his vision.

Reagan's predecessor, Jimmy Carter, was smarter and more diligent. Carter was also a micro-manager who even vetted requests to use the White House tennis courts. He survived one term and achieved relatively little.

As an entrepreneur you can follow Reagan's lead if:

- You have a very clear vision of what you want to do
- You build a great team to deliver the vision
- You focus your work on what you are best at doing and only you can do.

4. FOUNDER SYNDROME, AND HOW YOU CAN AVOID IT

As founder you will eat, breathe, sleep and dream your mission. It will take over your life and it will become a large part of your identity. Your charity will not just be a professional commitment, it will be an emotional calling. This can be hugely positive. Your passion will transmit itself to funders, stakeholders and team members. Stakeholders, funders and team members are more easily attracted to someone who is passionate about the cause than someone who is not. In the early days, your passion is the fuel which will help you overcome the many obstacles you will face. But passion is a two-sided coin: there is also an ugly side to it. Here are the seven deadly sins of founder syndrome:

1. *Intolerance of other people's views.* In starting up you will have had to overcome so many doubters and so many objections. Your success will have proven them all wrong. You will have plenty of evidence to show that your judgement is good and others have questionable judgement. But founders, unlike the Pope, are not infallible. Learn to listen and respect the views of your team. If you do not value their views, you do not value them as people and they will leave. And if you do not value the views of your board, you condemn yourself to conflict with them. At least pretend that you are interested in what they say.

2. *Inability to trust other people to perform.* You will have performed miracles, both major and minor, to start your charity. You cannot expect your team to be miracle workers as well. You should expect that they are professionals, not magicians. If you cannot trust your team to perform, you will avoid delegating to them. And when you do delegate, you will micro-manage them. Those are very good ways of showing that you do not trust your team. They will realize you do not trust them: motivation and performance will go down and there will be a parting of ways. You lose their talent and they lose their jobs: not good for anyone.

3. *Expecting others to have the same level of passion as you do.* No one will love your baby as much as you do. They will believe in the mission, but they also have lives to live. They will not sacrifice their entire life for you. You have to learn to moderate your demands of your team: they cannot do everything overnight.

4. *Inflated sense of ego and focus on promoting self.* As you succeed, you will attract both attention and admiration. Enjoy this, but not too much. It is much more interesting to

speak at conferences and get applause, appear on the media and get articles written about you; it is also very nice to sit on government commissions where you write important-sounding reports. You will persuade yourself that you are helping the mission by building profile and network. You are helping your ego, not your charity. Allow yourself two days a month for this profile work and stick to the day job for the rest of the time.

5. *Loss of interest in the day-to-day*. After some years, the routine humdrum of delivering the mission will seem... routine and humdrum. But your success came from the hard day-to-day grind of making things work. That is how you must sustain success. The huge risk is that the day-to-day grind becomes very boring. Within the organization, it is tempting to focus on the new and shiny stuff, not the dull and boring: ambitious new projects are more interesting but mean you lose focus on what matters. If you really want to do new things, that is a sign that you should move on and start a new mission elsewhere.

6. *Identity conflation*. You will naturally identify strongly with your charity and your mission. It will not just be your job, it will become your identity. It is your calling card in life. That in itself is dangerous because it makes it very hard for you to move on. More dangerously, over time the charity becomes identified with you. The cult of the hero leader can be very strong, both internally and externally. This strength can also be weakness: too much depends on you. The strength of the charity should be embedded in the team, not one person.

7. *Inability to move on*. Success can be your biggest enemy. The more you succeed, the harder it is to let go. Why on earth would you abandon a success story for which you are known? From experience you will know just how much risk and hard work it takes to start up. The more successful you become, the more you become trapped by your success. Do not let success become a prison: make it a platform for achieving even greater things elsewhere.

Founder syndrome is hard to avoid. It creeps up on you slowly and you will be the last person to recognize the symptoms. Unlike Julius Caesar in his moment of triumph, you will not have a slave to whisper in your ear, 'Remember you are human.' You are also unlikely to receive honest feedback from your team. People do not like to annoy their boss, or people who have power over them. All too often founder syndrome only comes into the open through a crisis or through the board taking matters into their own hands.

One way to avoid founder's syndrome is to set yourself very clear goals about what you want to achieve, and by when. When you achieve these goals, be ready to move on to your next venture. Goal clarity will give you a sense of urgency and focus. In practice, if you stay much more than seven years, you have stayed too long: you will find it hard to move on. And you should have achieved what you set out to achieve roughly within that time frame. There are exceptions to this: if you are attempting systems change at a global level (like Grameen or STIR Education), it will take you much longer to pilot, develop and then roll out globally the correct interventions.

KIDS COMPANY: WEAKNESS THROUGH STRENGTH*

Kids Company was founded by Camila Batmanghelidjh in 1996 to provide support to deprived inner-city children. With her large turbans and flamboyant dress, she was the face of the charity. She demonstrated huge passion and commitment in overcoming endless obstacles and made Kids Company one of the most prominent names in the sector. Camila was showered with honours: Social Entrepreneur of the Year in 2005, Woman of the Year in 2006 and a CBE from the Queen in 2013;

---

*This was widely covered in the media. See, for instance, the BBC, 7 August 2015. https://www.bbc.co.uk/news/uk-33822035

numerous honorary doctorates followed and she was a darling of the media.

Camila was able to mesmerize supporters and donors with her passion. Even the Prime Minister, David Cameron, appeared to be impressed by her. He and his ministers ignored the advice of civil servants and made a £3 million grant to Kids Company, just a few weeks before it had to close in 2015 amid a blitz of claims about ineffective management and poor value for money.

The collapse was sudden and dramatic. By sheer force of personality, Camila had created magic out of nothing. But over time, magic and force of personality are not enough. You need a professional team that is trusted, effective governance, proper management of finances, measurement of impact and a machine which can deliver reliably without the need for magic. Sadly, Camila died peacefully in her sleep, aged 61, in 2024.

Starting a charity and sustaining a charity are different skill sets. Over time you need to rely on the team and the machine, not on one person, however brilliant they may be. Relying on the founder to do it all can be a strength at the start but a weakness when you reach scale.

5. HOW TO RECRUIT A STRONG TEAM

However good you are, you are only as good as your team. And you are 100 per cent accountable for making sure that you have the right team and that it performs well. If your team is useless, do not blame them: look in the mirror. You recruited the team, you manage the team so their performance is your responsibility.

You need the best people if you are to achieve your mission. Not-for-profits focus on some of the toughest challenges facing the world: climate change, environment, education, human rights. And managing a not-for-profit is far harder than managing a for-profit firm. If the challenge is so hard and so important, you need the best people. The accusation that not-for-profit management are overpaid is wide of the mark: arguably, not-for-profit managers should be some of the highest paid people given the nature of the challenges they deal with. Instead, most work on very modest salaries. Fortunately, you can find great people out there who put a higher value on purpose than they do on profit.

In recruiting your team, you have five factors to work with:

- *Purpose*: why you can compete for the best talent
- *Value proposition*: how you can make your employment offer attractive
- *Skills mix*: what are the key skills you need?
- *Values*: how do you balance the need for skills with the need for good values?
- *Diversity*: diversity is not a goal, it is a benefit.

If you get these factors right, you should be able to recruit a team which can deliver.

Purpose

The recruitment challenge for charities is daunting. Unlike investment banks, you cannot throw money at people to attract them. But, like the investment banks, you need to be able to attract the top talent if you are to succeed. Running a charity should never mean settling for second best. Changing lives, changing the world is at least as important as making a profit. The biggest challenges in the world requires the best talent in the world.

Your definition of 'top' talent is likely to differ from that of an investment bank: you will want people with great ability and with great values. The people you want to recruit will have a sense of purpose or mission which extends beyond the desire for a trophy house and a trophy spouse. This is where all charities have a competitive advantage over employers who solve every problem with more money: you offer something which they cannot offer. You offer people a sense of purpose, which is increasingly compelling.

Mercer Consulting produced a report from over 7,000 HR professionals globally and found three factors which employees look for. The good news is that you can offer all of them:

- Permanent work flexibility
- Commitment to health and wellbeing
- A sense of purpose.

While many firms can offer the first two factors (although not all do), very few offer a sense of purpose. According to Mercer, only 13 per cent of firms offer a sense of purpose beyond profit. Where there is a sense of purpose, three times as many employees report that they thrive, which is good for morale, motivation, performance and retention. The Mercer 2024 Global Talent Trends Survey[*] shows that in most countries, pride in the purpose of the organization is the single most important factor in helping staff thrive at work. Purpose is vital and is hard-wired into the work of charities.

Value proposition
As much as you may interview potential employees, they are interviewing you as a potential employer too. You need to show that you can offer candidates an attractive value proposition. Part of that is a sense of purpose and we have seen above how work flexibility and commitment to health and wellbeing are demanded by over 80 per cent of candidates.

In the absence of large salaries, there are three ways you can build a compelling value proposition:

a) Career development
b) Autonomy and responsibility
c) Culture.

[*]https://www.mercer.com/insights/people-strategy/future-of-work/global-talent-trends/ Page 24.

a) *Career development.* Jobs for life have gone and average tenure with an employer is now under six years,[*] and significantly less for recent graduates. You can make a virtue of this by framing your organization as a three- to five-year career accelerator. Show how staff gain skills, experience and training which will enable them to go on to great things elsewhere. Make a virtue out of the reality that you will never grow fast enough to satisfy the promotion expectations of everyone you recruit: you need people to move on.

b) *Autonomy and responsibility.* It is hard to think that you are changing the world if you are a cog in a machine. But if you have a small organization, you can show how each person has real responsibility and autonomy: this is what many people crave. The implication of having autonomy and responsibility is that you have to perform. In a small organization, you cannot carry passengers. Implicitly, you need to foster high expectations and a performance culture.

c) *Culture.* You can offer a unique culture. For instance, in India we found that many staff were used to a very hierarchical and deferential business culture so we made a virtue out of not being hierarchical or deferential. In daring to be different, we were able to recruit great talent which fitted our way of working.

Skills mix

You need to do far more than recruit programme delivery talent. You must recruit the capability to run and grow the organization. This is where founders have the same blind spot as funders – both

---

[*]OECD: https://stats.oecd.org/Index.aspx?DataSetCode=TENURE_FREQ. This average disguises the real pattern: tenure increases dramatically with age. New graduates stay under two years typically; as they find work that suits them, they stay longer.

hate spending on overhead. But functions like IT, finance and HR are not overhead. They are the functions which will help you run the organization smoothly. Perhaps the greatest sin is failing to invest properly in finance and accounting. It is easy to dislike accounting because it is dry, technical and seems to add no value to your mission. But if you do not have a good accounting function you are at risk: you will not have adequate controls to protect you from fraud and waste nor adequate insight to manage cash flow and manage budgets well. Failing to invest in finance and accounting can lead to you going out of business. You cannot change the world if you are bankrupt. So if you hate accounting, learn to love accountants: they may just save you from disaster.

As with finance and accounting, so too with the other functions. If you are to run a successful and professional organization, you need all the support that IT, finance, accounting, legal and HR can give you.

If you think of support functions as overhead, you will not invest properly. Do not ask 'how much should I spend on overhead?' because the answer will always be zero. Reframe the question. Ask 'how much should I invest in building capacity?' Spending and overhead is bad, but investment and capacity are good. They are, of course, the same thing. Investing in the right support frees up your front-line staff to focus on what they do best: delivery.

Values
I had been talking to a CEO about his HR strategy and it was a predictable conversation about the challenges all firms face. At the end of the interview he relaxed and as I was leaving, he said, 'It's odd, isn't it? I find I hire people for their skills and fire them for their [lack of] values.'

In that one moment the CEO summed up an eternal truth of hiring and firing: we hire for skills and fire for values, normally. This is the wrong way round because you can always train skills, but you can never train values.

VALUES OR SKILLS?

Timpson is a chain of shoe repair shops in the UK. They are not glamorous places to work and the pay is not great. What would you look for when hiring people to work there? John Timpson, the founder, started with the obvious solution: he looked for cobblers. They were a disaster: cobblers could deal with shoes, not people. Cobblers prefer soles to souls.

Timpson realized that he could train people to repair shoes easily, but he could not train cobblers to be positive, enthusiastic customer service people.* So he told his area managers to start recruiting to values, not skills. They did not get it, because they felt safer recruiting cobblers. Eventually, Timpson replaced the wordy evaluation form with a sheet of paper which had a series of cartoons on it. On the positive side was Mr Keen, Mr Reliable, Miss Helpful, Mrs Determined and other good stereotypes. On the other side was Mr Grumpy, Mr Rude, Ms Late, Miss Fib.[†] The area managers simply had to identify which type the candidate was like and make the hiring decision on that basis. Managers started hiring to values and then trained people to repair shoes. The Timpson chain has never looked back and is now the market leader.

You can train skills, but not values. Hire to values.

Diversity
Much ink has been spilled on the moral and ethical case for diversity. By now, most people understand that diversity is socially and morally desirable but in reality, your goal is not to achieve diversity. Your goal is to deliver your mission. But does diversity enhance performance?

*Original conversation with the author.
[†]*The Happy Index: Lessons in Upside-Down Management*, James Timpson (HarperCollins, 2024). Summary with the Mr Men here: https://harpercollins.co.uk/blogs/features/management -strategies-hiring-the-right-people

In practice, there are two types of diversity which are vital in helping you achieve your goals:

- Diversity of thinking
- Diversity of age and experience.

Diversity of thinking. Many firms tout proudly that they are 'one-firm firms' and claim that they embrace diversity. In practice, this means you can be any race, colour, creed or gender as long as you sign up to a single set of values, a common way of thinking and of doing things. That is not diversity in any useful sense. It is a way to encourage conformity and group think. If you are to solve highly complex and dynamic systems problems, you need as much diversity of perspective and thinking as you can. In practice, this probably means you need people from different backgrounds, with different experience and different skills. They probably will have diversity of colour, creed and gender but they will not have conformity of thought.

Diversity of age and experience. The importance of this became clear when we started Teach First: there was a huge gap in approach between the experienced board and the inexperienced executive. The experienced board could see all the hazards we would face and constantly urged caution. Their favourite phrase was 'over reach'. This was their code for saying that we were being too ambitious and taking too many risks. The youthful executive had no idea that what we were doing was impossible so we went ahead and did it anyway. When we wanted someone to attend our first birthday party, we called Downing Street and got the Prime Minister to come. Had we listened to advice we would have realized that it was impossible to get a prime minister to turn up to an event for a new charity with no track record, but equally the board stopped us doing some really dumb things.

Diversity of age and experience is shorthand for saying that you need a balance of people who are ambitious and risk taking, and those who have experience and can help you avoid the biggest risks and mistakes. It is a vital form of diversity of thinking.

6. HOW YOUR TEAM HAS TO CHANGE AS YOU GROW

As your organization grows it follows an inevitable path of professionalization. What this means in practice is:

- More specialization of roles: you will need specialists, not generalists.
- More robust systems and process: you will need stronger finance, accounting and budget systems, better controls, clearer HR policies and procedures (pay, promotion, performance management), clear rhythms and routines for reporting and communication.
- More formal decision making: less ad hoc decision making, more focus on proper data and analysis with adequate input from a range of experts and stakeholders.

This means that the team you start with is unlikely to be the team that takes you to scale. At the start, you need people who are highly entrepreneurial, are comfortable with ambiguity and risk, and they like to have autonomy and responsibility. These people hate the path to professionalization. They see it as the creeping, dead hand of bureaucracy taking over and crushing their precious creation. If done badly, the path to professionalization can be the path to bureaucracy.

In practice, the crunch comes when you reach somewhere between 40 to 80 staff. When you have less than 40 staff, you can organize informally and on an ad hoc basis, because everyone more or less knows what everyone else is doing. By the time you have 80 staff, it is impossible for everyone to know what everyone else is doing: this is when you need systems to replace personal knowledge and relationships. This is a challenging time for a growing organization. One by one, members of your founding team will come to you and tell you that you are destroying the magic which built your charity. These people, who will have been through hell for you, will then resign in disgust or despair. It is hard for them and for you but the brutal reality is that both they and the charity need to move on: you cannot avoid the need to professionalize and they cannot avoid the need to work in a startup.

The good news is that as you grow, it becomes easier to hire skilled staff. Your job descriptions become more focused, which in turn makes it easier to target the right specialist skills you need. As you grow, candidates will start to see you as a safer career option. You will expand your pool of potential candidates. You will lose the entrepreneurial skills of the startup team, but gain the professional skills you need for scale.

7. HOW TO MANAGE YOUR TEAM

Many founders are accidental managers: they are people who never intended to become managers and may have no experience of managing a team. If this is the case, you are not alone. The corporate world is full of accidental managers. It is also full of experienced managers who have never had any training in how to manage a team and they do not know how to manage a team. In practice, research[*] shows that there are five things your team most wants from you:

- Vision
- Motivation
- Decisiveness
- Strength in a crisis
- Honesty.

Deliver on the big five and you are well on the path to being a good manager. Here they are, in order:

Vision. The good news is that you will have a vision. It is likely to be a vision with a purpose that goes beyond profit. This puts you in a good position and far ahead of most managers in the corporate world. But to make your vision really powerful, show how each person can

[*]Proprietary research initially conducted on behalf of Teach First by the author and first published in *How to Lead* 1e, 2006.

contribute to your vision. Make your vision personal to them, rather than just an abstract ideal. Once people see how they can make a difference, they will want to make a difference.

Motivation. Two-thirds of bosses rate themselves well on motivation, but only a third of team members agree. There is a reality gap here. While many books have been written on motivation, we found one question consistently differentiated motivational bosses from the rest. Here is the golden question: 'My boss cares for me and my career' (agree/disagree on a five-point scale). Take an interest in each team member and show that you care: it's that simple. Caring does not mean offering perks or being nice, it can mean having difficult but constructive conversations with them about performance and development. It means respecting them as individuals and it can even mean saying 'thank you' once in a while. A little recognition goes a long way.

Decisiveness. A good way to demotivate a team is to delay decisions, be unclear about what you want and then change your mind. That will maximize uncertainty and rework, and will guarantee frustration. Decisiveness is not about being an autocrat. It is about ensuring decisions are made (by you or others) promptly, clearly and with the right involvement of the right people. It means being clear not only about what needs to happen and how and when; it means being clear about *why* the decision matters. Only when your team understands the context and the trade-offs can they really understand the decision properly. They will understand not by communication after the decision has been made, but by involving them appropriately before the decision is made.

Strength in a crisis. Crises are the moments where leaders step up and followers step back. This is where you prove your worth. As a leader, you will need to drive your team to action, not analysis. But your team will remember how you act even more than what you do. In a crisis, the leader has to be the purveyor of hope, certainty and clarity, even if you feel fear, doubt and confusion internally. You need to be positive and solution focused so that others remain positive and solution focused. This is the time to wear the mask of leadership: be the leader that you would want to follow.

Honesty. Honesty for leaders is not about ethics and morality. It is far more important than that. Honesty is about trust and it is highly divisive. If there is lack of trust between team and leader, either the team leaves or the leader leaves. Trust is about doing as you say. Most of us think we do as we say. The problem is rarely in the doing, the problem is nearly always in what we say. When asked to do something we may say things like 'I will try... I will look into it... I will see what I can do... I will do my best...' We are clearly not committing. But what is heard is different to what is said: what is heard is 'I will do it.' So, when you come back two weeks later and say, 'I looked into it and it was not possible,' you will have done as you said and you will have lost all trust. There will then be a long and tedious 'I said you said but she meant and I thought why didn't you...' discussion which simply destroys more trust. And trust is like a vase: once broken, it is very hard to put back together again.

You need to be trusted as a leader. That means you must be crystal clear about expectations. It is better to have a difficult conversation early about expectations than to have an impossible conversation at the end about what went wrong.

When you start up, your leadership and team management will be highly personal because you will know and manage everyone on your small team. At this early stage, these five principles of team management will be enough for you to manage well. But as your organization grows, you will need to professionalize the management of the team. You will need clearer HR systems: clear performance management, appraisals, objectives, development plans, HR handbooks and compensation plans. These systems should assure fairness and transparency. But however large your organization grows, you will still need the five qualities of a good leader: vision, motivation, decisiveness, strength in a crisis and honesty.

PEOPLE: SUMMARY

The founder

The most important person, for you and your idea, is yourself. Evidence shows that you do not need to be a genius, have an MBA or be a brilliant leader. You need a good idea and the passion to pursue it.

The best way to start is carefully. Explore your idea and slowly build your support while you still have a job. Then leap when you know you have a good idea, a good team and some sources of initial funding. As your NGO grows, so your role changes. You have to learn to let go and trust your team. Focus your time on less and less, which normally means: managing external stakeholders and managing the top team. Your title never changes, but your job does. You have to keep on promoting yourself in role.

At some point, find the courage to step out and hand over. You should not become dependent on the NGO (and the NGO should not remain dependent on you). Success comes when it can thrive without you.

The team

You are as good as your team. Recruit the best you can find and if in doubt, hire to values, not skills: you can train skills, not values.

As you grow, your team will change from being entrepreneurial jacks of all trades to more skilled and specialized professionals. The transition from entrepreneurial to professional is traumatic and eventually most of your startup team will leave.

The best way to manage your team is to trust them as professionals. If you have recruited well then you can delegate, not micro-manage.

4

Partnerships

Build the coalitions which will take your idea to scale

Discover how partnerships can help you achieve the breadth and scope of intervention required to change the world. This chapter shows how you can work with other actors to develop an integrated solution to a complex problem: you don't have to do it all yourself.

Partnerships are like liquorice allsorts: they come in all sorts, sizes and flavours. Each partnership presents different opportunities and challenges. This chapter will focus on four types of partner who can help you succeed. These partners are:

- *Government*
- *Funders*
- *Private Sector*
- *Other NGOs.*

INTRODUCTION

If you want to change the world, you have to change a highly complex and ever shifting system. Changing the world single-handedly is heroic and impossible. Even heroes need an army of supporters to help them. In the past, you had to build your own vast army to succeed. Now you have to work with other people's armies:

you focus on what you are best at doing and they focus on what they are best at doing. The good news is that you no longer need scale to succeed. The bad news is that making partnerships work is hard and full of pitfalls.

Partnerships can help you achieve scale as well as scope: partnerships for scale were covered in the chapter on Impact. Scale partnerships are simpler because you are combining the efforts of organizations who share the same goal. Partnerships for scope are harder because you are combining organizations who have different agendas and priorities, even if they are working on the same system. For instance, if you want to help an offender stop re-offending on release from prison, you may need to deal with housing, employment, skills, literacy, mental health, substance abuse and many other issues. Different organizations may be excellent at dealing with one of those issues: partnerships for scope are about integrating all these initiatives. Each organization has a different skill and different focus but they have a common goal: reduce re-offending. They cannot succeed alone, they can only succeed together.

This chapter shows how four different sorts of partner can help you achieve the breadth of intervention to change highly complex systems:

- Government
- Funders
- Private Sector
- Other NGOs.

GOVERNMENT

NGOs have a love–hate relationship with government: they love the money but hate the bureaucracy and restrictions. Both the love and the hate are entirely unreciprocated by government: they simply want to find a way of meeting their policy objectives. The balance of power is unequal: they can live without you, but you may find it hard to live without them.

At first sight, it seems impossible to have a real partnership when there is such a power imbalance between the two parties. But in practice, NGOs are able to do things which governments cannot do. This means that, despite the scale difference, governments need good NGOs. Where there is mutual dependency, there is the opportunity for a real partnership. To develop a partnership, you have to see the world through the eyes of your partner: identify where you fit into their world and where they depend on you.

The biggest mistake you can make is to fall in love with your own idea. This will make you a great advocate for your idea, but it can also blind you. It can stop you seeing the world through the eyes of your potential partner. For instance, we were meeting the prisons minister to discuss a programme to help offenders into self-employment on release from prison. The founder was evangelical about the wonders of self-employment which led to minimal re-offending. She harangued the minister at length about his failure to have a self-employment programme and the meeting ended in some acrimony.

The minister was not against re-offending, but he saw the world differently. He wanted to trial a large-scale programme which would join up self-employment with employment and other services for offenders. In other words, he was ready to offer us a much larger opportunity than the one we had been thinking about. The founder could not see beyond her own, brilliant intervention. The best way to see the world through your partner's eyes is to listen. All the best leaders and sales people are like the best communicators: they have two ears and one mouth. And they use them in that proportion: they listen twice as much as they talk.

There are three roles which NGOs can play, which let them do things which governments struggle to do. These roles can help you create mutual dependency and create a good partnership:

1. Innovator
2. Contractor
3. Trusted partner.

In each of these roles you will see common themes emerge:

- Understand the needs of government by listening closely;
- Align your offering with what they need, while not compromising on your mission;
- Build trust by setting expectations clearly, always delivering and communicating well;
- Manage risk, especially the risk of over-dependency on a few officials or ministers.

Here, we will briefly explore how you can use each of the three roles of an NGO to build a relationship with government.

Innovator
Governments are not known for being hotbeds of entrepreneurial zeal, for good reason. They cannot be seen to be taking risks with taxpayers' money and with citizens' lives. This gives governments a problem which NGOs can solve: governments need a steady flow of new ideas so that they can improve delivery of services. NGOs can be a rich source of new ideas.

Many NGOs essentially remediate a failure in government policy. They identify a problem and pilot a solution. When you identify one problem, it often leads to finding another, as the example below illustrates.

INNOVATING TO FIX GOVERNMENT POLICY FAILURES

Teach First was set up because the government could not find great graduates to teach in the most challenging schools. The schemes government came up with were hopeless. One promised graduates a free laptop if they joined the programme. Any graduate who chooses their future career on the basis of a free laptop needs their head examining. Teach First came up with a proposition tailored to the needs of top graduates.

Teach First then discovered that the success of its participants depended heavily on the quality of the head teacher, but government could not get great head teachers to teach in the most challenging schools. So we set up Future Leaders to identify and prepare great head teachers. The programme was wholly original and successful.

We then realized that the success of Head Teachers depended heavily on the quality of their middle management: the heads of year and heads of subject departments. But government programmes ignored middle management, perhaps because it was too boring: it lacked the glamour of fresh new graduates and the power of head teachers. So we created Teaching Leaders to build a completely new approach to developing middle managers. We finally realized (15 years after starting Teach First) that the management programmes should be integrated, so we merged Teaching Leaders and Future Leaders to create Ambition Institute.

Meanwhile, the graduates of Teach First kept on identifying other failures in government policy. Outside education, they created NGOs to get great graduates into social work (Front Line), the police force (Police Now) and into the prisons service (Unlocked). Within education graduates identified the need for better support for improving whole towns' prospects (Right to Succeed), improving oracy (Voice21) and to give voice to the efforts of all the charities addressing educational inequality, they created the Fair Education Alliance, which now has nearly 300 members.[*]

Creating one charity has spawned over 20 other charities. Once you identify one challenge, you will quickly start to find many more. You cannot address them all yourself, but you can address them as part of a network of like-minded organizations: there is never a lack of problems which governments need to solve.

[*]June 2024. https://www.faireducation.org.uk/alliance-members

NGOs play a vital role as the innovation lab for government. You can try things and take risks in a way that government cannot. If your innovation does not work, then you have a problem but the government does not. If your innovation works, both you and the government have a problem: what do you do next?

Some NGOs set themselves up explicitly to innovate an idea and then 'sell' it to government: let government take the idea and integrate it into their delivery. This is essentially what Teach First, Teaching Leaders and Future Leaders did. They proved the concept and then got government to fund its expansion. This is highly risky, because it puts the NGO at the mercy of officials and ministers. Relying on government leads to four major problems:

- Policy
- Procurement
- Value for money
- Contract administration.

Policy: ministers change and so do priorities. What matters today may not matter tomorrow. The moment you fall out of favour, you are finished. The obvious point is that you need to nurture your political networks, both within government and with opposition parties. You never know who will be in office next. Less obviously, you have to have a network of supporters among officials who can give you early warning about policy changes, opportunities and pitfalls. One official warned me that the government was under pressure to make cuts, so they were going to cut the programmes which were easy to cut. Note: they would not cut big bad programmes, which could be difficult. They would make easy cuts: that meant cutting low-profile programmes like ours, which no one would notice. So we spent six months making our programme very high profile: we went from being easy to cut, to being hard to cut. We survived. Always make sure you understand the agenda from the perspective of ministers and officials.

118

Procurement: you will find yourself in the odd position of having to bid for the right to deliver your own programme. If you lose, you are finished. The traditional way of managing this is to make friends with the officials and then write the tender document with them. If you write the tender well, it will precisely reflect what you do and all your strengths: it will be impossible for anyone else to submit a competitive bid.

Value for money: civil servants are under constant pressure to deliver value for money. They normally focus on the money and not on the value, because it is easier to prove that you have cut costs than it is to prove you have increased value. Even if you win the right to deliver your own programme, you will have to endure death by a thousand budget cuts. At first you can find efficiency savings, then you can find innovative ways of delivering better. Finally, you have to cut too far and the programme suffers. At that point, the civil servants deem the programme to be ineffective and you are finished. Only sustained lobbying of ministers and officials over many years can delay, but not avoid, this fate.

Contract administration: to manage risk, officials tend to overspecify. This makes it impossible to innovate within the contract, or to improve outcomes or reduce costs. We have even had civil servants mandating which PowerPoint slides should be used in which training sessions. This can only be avoided if you have worked with officials during the procurement process: make sure that the tender is written in such a way that you will be allowed flexibility in how you deliver the outcomes.

If you are an innovation lab for government, you perform a vital role for society. Your real challenge will not come if your innovation fails, because you will remain in control of your fate: you can either try something new or you can fold. The real challenge is knowing what to do if you succeed. You will then need to partner with government to take your idea to scale and that is never easy. To make the most of your chances, you will have to:

- Build and maintain a strong network of sympathetic and influential officials
- Move swiftly to align your agenda with that of any incoming minister
- Ensure that you shape any tenders which affect you, so that you can win them.

This may sound like intensely political work and it is intensely political. If you want to change the world, you have to engage with power at some point.

Contractor
The challenge for government is that they cannot deal with 300 small and innovative charities to fix each policy priority. The challenges of integration, quality control and administration are simply too great. Instead, government prefers to deal with large contractors who can do all necessary integration, quality control and risk management for them. The large contractors may be relatively slow, expensive and unimaginative, but they are safe: no one gets fired for hiring one of the big-name contractors.

Clearly, you can attempt to become a large contractor for government but this is likely to result in you losing your focus and mission. To survive as a contractor, you need a portfolio of contracts. If you lose one contract, you need to be able to pick up other contracts. You will have to chase the money to survive. Unlike the innovator who proactively takes an agenda to government, you will reactively respond to whatever agenda and tenders the government decides to pursue. You will land up having a business but not a mission.

The more likely outcome is that you will have to grow your idea by working with one of the large contractors who work with government. If you do this, you are no longer in control of your destiny. You can hope to get lucky and find a good contractor to work with, but good large contractors are very rare. Most simply seek to maximize profit and minimize risk.

There are two ways in which you may find yourself as a sub-contractor. Government may find it too risky to deal with a small startup, so they will place the contract through an established contractor to oversee your delivery. The main contractor may well decide to take 40 per cent of the contract value for the joy of overseeing your work, which has just become much harder because you have just forfeited 40 per cent of your budget. The second way in which you land up as a sub-contractor is when you are delivering one part of a much larger contract which the contractor has won. The main contractor may genuinely rely on your specialist skills, or may have simply included you in the bid as some window dressing: the contract may have required them to show that they are working with diverse, small and innovative organizations to win the contract.

Life as a subcontractor is not comfortable. Typical complaints about the main contractor include allegations that they:

- Force all the delivery risk on to you and make payment conditional on delivery of results. This leads to serious cash flow challenges.
- Take a large top slice of the budget (40 per cent), or simply allocate you minimal budget.
- Put in place onerous reporting requirements to protect themselves from challenge by government. This often enables them to delay payments until every reporting requirement has been completed, documented and fully audited.
- Delay payments to fund their own cash flow requirements.
- Forbid you to talk to government, making it impossible for you to develop your own agenda with government or to complain about the poor treatment you are receiving.
- Steal your Intellectual Property and use it, often in debased form which tarnishes your reputation.

Even if you hire good lawyers to help you negotiate the contract with the main contractor, the reality is that they have the money and you do not. They are largely able to dictate terms to you: you can either agree to the terms or have no contract. The four ways to ameliorate this are:

- Find a contractor you can trust and bid for the contract with them. Ideally, this allows you to shape the scale and scope of your role during the bidding process. This helps you develop a worthwhile contract with a partner you trust.
- Have a strong relationship with government and have government specify that any winning contractor must use your intervention. Contractors hate this because it means you have power and access, but that is their problem. You can normally only achieve this outcome if you have a unique offering which government recognizes has high value.
- Have a unique and essential service which the main contractor has to use to deliver their contract. This creates mutual dependency and shifts power in your direction. You have to use this power in contract negotiations to make sure you get the right contract.

Working for government as a main contractor makes it hard to stay mission focused and is hard to achieve. Working for government as a sub-contractor is rarely satisfactory in terms of economics or outcomes. In reality, it is normally a last resort partnership.

Of all the ways of partnering with government, becoming a contractor or sub-contractor is probably the choice of last resort. Being a contractor means loss of true mission focus, being a sub-contractor means that you are likely to get screwed.

Trusted partner

As a contractor or innovator you are an outsider who remains on the outside. As a trusted partner, you are still an outsider, but you start acting and working on the inside. As trusted partner, you no longer try to deliver the mission for the government; you deliver it with the government. Government takes responsibility, with you, for delivering the outcomes. This is a transformational relationship because it dramatically increases the accountability, involvement and commitment of the government to your cause.

This trusted partner role is different from being an activist who demands that government takes action on your behalf. You remain involved and committed in delivering results. Your involvement will involve both advice and action. If only you (not government) take action, then the government will have no skin in the game: they will feel no accountability for your programme and your programme will last only so long as you fund it yourself. That is not a sustainable model. If you only offer advice, then you are like any other lobby group that advises government. The credibility of your advice comes from the success of your action.

Becoming a trusted partner involves both advice and action. Taking action shows your commitment and demonstrates what is possible. It is also your research lab to find out what is possible in the local context. You are creating a viable template for the government to adopt. The purpose of offering advice is to embed your programme in government so that they own the programme and will continue it at scale: you do not need to fund and run the programme yourself.

IMAZON: HELPING THE COMMUNITY TO SAVE ITS FOREST*

Imazon set itself the challenge of reducing deforestation in the Amazon. This is a highly complex challenge involving national and local government, local communities, ranchers, indigenous people, different economic interests and complex ecology. They contributed one vital piece of this jigsaw puzzle: independent and trusted data.

---

*Erin Worsham, Catherine Clark, and Robyn Fehrman, May 2017. Imazon: Using Data and Partnerships to Save the Amazon. Innovation Investment Alliance and CASE at Duke. Scaling Pathways.

Imazon ran an early pilot, from 2010, in Paragominas municipality. Although it only has a population of 111,000, it covers the size of Belgium. How can so few people know what is happening over such a large area? Imazon solved the problem by providing reliable and up-to-date satellite tracking of what was happening on the ground. Local officials did not even know if or where deforestation was continuing in their forest.

But data alone was not enough. Federal regulations aimed at stopping deforestation had led to conflict locally so Imazon used its trusted partner status to convene the local stakeholders. This enabled them to reach fair decisions on what was legal and illegal logging, and on licensing and enforcement of rules. These groups were able to identify and share more sustainable farming practices. Good data also made it easier to create an accurate registry of land ownership and control, which also made enforcement easier.

The results of the pilot were a 90 per cent decrease in deforestation and widespread acceptance of more sustainable farming and forestry practices. In theory, Imazon only held one small piece of the deforestation jigsaw. They used that to become a trusted partner to local government and the community. As a trusted partner, it was able to get the municipal government to embed practices which reduced deforestation. Ownership of the programme lay with government, not with Imazon. That makes the programme self-sustaining over time and Imazon continues to play the trusted partner role as the independent data provider.

What works at the pilot stage does not always scale. Imazon reported in 2024* that forest clearance has been at record levels for five years in a row across the Amazon. Local partnerships ensured the success of the pilot locally; delivering the required national partnerships has been harder.

---

*Imazon Activity report 2022–33, published May 2024. https://imazon.org.br/en/publicacoes/activity-report-2022-3/

The trusted partner model is highly attractive because it is:

- Sustainable over time: the government is committed to continuing the programme.
- Sustainable economically: Imazon has a budget of c $5 million a year to cover Brazil; STIR has a budget of $3 million to reach 6 million children.
- High impact: outcomes are enhanced when government takes accountability for the programme and its results.
- Mission focused: as a trusted partner, you can remain focused on delivering the one piece of the jigsaw where you have a genuine core competence. You can deal with a complex issue with wide scope without mission drift or loss of focus.

But achieving trusted partner status is not easy. You have to put in place the following conditions:

- A credible intervention with demonstrable effect and a sound track record: know your magic sauce and understand what you bring to the party.
- Understanding of, and alignment with, the agenda of government officials. Respect their needs, not just yours.
- A relatively stable and competent government that has the capacity to sustain an intervention.
- Good relationships with government officials, especially at senior levels.
- Patient funders who understand that putting these conditions in place takes years, not months.

Many NGOs like to pretend that they have a trusted partner relationship with their host government. But in truth, they are trusted only for as long as the money keeps flowing into the coffers of government and, all too often, into the pockets of officials. You will know you have reached trusted partner status when:

- Officials call you for help and advice, you do not have to call them
- They want to sustain your programme with their time, money and resources
- You hear in advance about their plans and potential bidding opportunities, and you get the chance to shape those plans and opportunities.

It takes time and effort to build this level of relationship. Once you have built the relationship, you have to keep on investing in the relationship and sustaining trust. Never take the relationship for granted. If you build a trusted partner relationship, that is an investment which will pay great dividends for you and your mission.

FUNDERS

The relationship between funders and the funded (NGOs, charities) is often unsatisfactory. Funders resent being treated as piggy banks. NGOs are driven crazy by the reporting requirements and restrictions which funders put on their grants. Here, we will look at this relationship from three perspectives:

1. Grantees: NGOs and charities
2. Funders: donors and philanthropists
3. The future perfect partnership.

1. Grantees: NGOs and charities.

Traditionally, charities treat funders like teenagers treat parents: they like the money and support but they resent the control. This is a dysfunctional relationship for both parties. The funders clearly have a need to know that their funds are being spent in the way that they want.

Funders are different from private sector funders. In the private sector, if a firm raises money then it will be for the executive to decide how to invest it. You would not expect the bank or shareholders to say that you can spend it only on labour and materials and you cannot spend it on HR, or marketing or finance. But in the not-for-profit sector, this is exactly what happens. Funders do not trust grantees to spend their money well, so funders tell grantees exactly what they can and cannot do with their money. Typically, they will try to avoid funding things like HR, marketing, IT or finance because they see that as overhead. Not many firms would survive without HR, marketing, IT or finance. Funders essentially ask charities to perform with one arm tied behind their back.

The challenge of restricted funding is a burden for most charities. From the point of view of the funder, restricted funding makes some sense. It requires that the funds you receive be spent on a particular purpose, which seems reasonable from their perspective. This causes five problems for charities, in ascending order of importance:

- Onerous reporting requirements
- Lack of funds to build capacity
- Mission creep
- Inhibits innovation
- Attacking symptoms, not causes of problems.

Onerous reporting requirements. Each item of spending and every hour spent has to be tracked and then allocated to different budgets from different funders. Inevitably, there will be grey areas where it is not clear which funder should be funding which person's time, especially as each individual will probably be spending time on different projects.

Every funder has their own needs in terms of what data needs to be presented in what format over what time period. The funder will not just want accounting data, they will legitimately ask for data on impact and outcomes in the format they expect. If you have 25 donors all asking for their own bespoke reporting requirements once a quarter, the charity drowns in red tape. What seems reasonable as an individual request from one funder becomes an impossible burden when multiplied up by 25.

Lack of funds to build capacity. No one wants to pay for overhead, everyone wants to pay for results. Funders will fund direct programme delivery, but do their very best to avoid paying for any overhead. If they do make allowance for overhead, it tends to be minimal. But if you want to fund a health intervention in the middle of the bush, you cannot just pay for the cost of the vaccination. You have to pay for someone to go to the middle of the bush; they have to be recruited and trained; they need transport; they will need to be able to report back accurately to satisfy the funder's reporting needs, which means IT and telecoms support; you will need good financial and control systems to avoid fraud, ensure the money is well spent and report back to the funder; you will need fundraisers to raise the money for the programme and you will need people to source the vaccinations and ensure their quality; you need people to design the programme, monitor its effectiveness and manage the organization. In other words, you need overhead to deliver a programme. The direct cost of the vaccine is trivial, the cost of getting it to the right arm in the right place in the right way is huge.

Failure to invest leads to the nonprofit starvation cycle.[*] Failure to invest in overhead means:

- Financial controls are weak and nonprofits are easy prey for fraudsters and waste.
- IT is not fit for purpose, productivity is weak and reporting is unreliable.
- Fundraising lacks capacity to raise enough resources to sustain the mission.
- HR systems are weak, leading to poor practices, little training, disaffected staff and high turnover, which is costly.
- No investment in learning, testing new ideas.

[*]Gregory, A.G. & Howard, D. (2009). The Nonprofit Starvation Cycle, Stanford Social Innovation Review, 7(4), 49–53. https://doi.org/10.48558/6K3V-0Q70

- No rainy day fund to fall back on when the unexpected happens, like a global pandemic.

In practice, this means that charities go to great lengths to develop sources of unrestricted income, which are like gold dust. Charities can spend unrestricted income as they wish, which enables them to build the capacity (overhead) to deliver the programmes which funders want.

Mission creep. Charities have no option but to chase the money. If you have no money, you have nothing. Chasing the money is a constant problem for charities. If you stay too focused on your core mission, you may well find it hard to raise enough funds to sustain the charity, but if you chase the money too hard, you will find that you stray further and further from your core mission. It is a very hard choice to make. For instance, one education charity* was offered a five-year grant to expand into Northern Nigeria. Economically, it would have been transformational: it would have secured the financial future of the charity and given it the base from which to build future operations. The executive was understandably keen to take the offer. The board declined the money, for two reasons: first, operating in Northern Nigeria represented security and corruption risks which it lacked experience to handle; second, the nature of the programme was too far from its core mission.

Inhibits innovation. If you want to win a grant, you have to show that you have something that works and has impact. So far, so sensible. The funder naturally wants to make sure that their funds have the desired impact and so they restrict the use of their funds to the initiative which works. This still appears to make sense, unless every funder has the same idea. If funders only fund what already works, then that crowds out any opportunity for innovation. But NGOs

*This charity remains anonymous at their request. Author's original research.

can only improve if they try new things and they can only solve the complex problems of the world if they innovate. Restricted funding pays for today but impoverishes the future.

Attacking symptoms, not causes of problems. Results focus sounds rational, but it has perverse effects. If you want to improve literacy, it sounds sensible to fund a reading programme. But that may tackle the symptom, not the cause of the problem. The real problem may not be that the current reading programme is deficient. It might be that teachers don't turn up, or are not motivated or not skilled. Or perhaps the problem is that children don't turn up because they have to work to feed their family; or perhaps girls don't turn up because there are no latrines and they are unsafe on the walk to and from school. In this case, funding a reading programme may lead to improvements to a small number of children who are already benefiting from a reasonable education, but it will completely miss the majority of children who have no access to education.

Addressing systemic problems requires patient funding that will drive innovation, build partnerships and develop sustainable solutions. Results focus is good for a quick fix, but not for lasting impact.

2. Funders: donors and philanthropists

Earning money is hard, but giving money should be easy, shouldn't it? Giving money badly is very easy, but giving it well is very hard. In practice, funders suffer from the same sorts of problems as the charities they fund: they are highly fragmented and are dealing with highly fragmented partners; they have limited resources; they can only fix one part of the solution they are facing.

Even the largest funders face the challenges of scale and fragmentation. The Bill and Melinda Gates Foundation has been making epic efforts to reduce malaria and they are one of the richest foundations in the world with over $50 billion of assets. But even they 'recognize that we are just one small part of a broader, global fight. That's why we work closely with partners to maximize the impact of our aggregate efforts." Just like no single charity can do it all alone, so too can no funder do it all alone.

But the obstacles to collaboration are high. Each foundation has its own board of trustees who have to make sure that the objects of the foundation are met. That means grant officers face perverse incentives which they pass on to the charities they fund:

- Avoid collaboration: show that your funding has achieved real results. If you pool resources with other charities, you cannot show causality from your funding to the end result.
- Focus on results which leads to quick fixes addressing symptoms not underlying causes. This lets the grants officer report back on successes to the board.
- Restrict funding: do not let your charities waste your money on overhead, then wonder why they lack the capacity to innovate or raise their game.
- Demand detailed reporting so that you can prove to your board that you are achieving value for money. You also need to show that you are mitigating the risk of fraud and waste. This raises the administrative and overhead burden on your charity.

All of this is a tragedy, in the way the ancient Greeks would have understood it. There is no villain, it is simply that the system (or in ancient Greece, capricious gods) conspires to force the heroes and heroines to act in ways that lead to disaster. Funders and the funded are all trying to do the right things for the right reasons, but find themselves forever rolling a huge stone up an endless mountain.

Both funders and the funded are locked in a dysfunctional and sub-optimal relationship which prevents systemic change being achieved. Can this be changed?

˙https://www.gatesfoundation.org/What-We-Do/Global-Health/Malaria

3. The future perfect partnership

In the future perfect, both funders and grantees need to up their game. The main features of the future perfect will involve some combination of:

- Partnership between funders and the funded, which reach beyond short-term restricted funding for specific projects.
- More collaboration between funders to address systemic issues and to force more collaboration between charities, governments and other stakeholders.
- Partnership with host governments which is not about giving them money, but involves the host government taking ownership of the programme and sustaining it over the long term.

The future perfect is not a pipe dream. The traditional ways of giving are starting to be challenged by trust-based philanthropy.[*] Trust-based philanthropy differs significantly from traditional philanthropy:[†]

- Unrestricted grants versus restricted. This enables charities to invest in building capacity and to pivot when the unexpected happens (such as the pandemic).
- Build relationships which go beyond money. Funders often have expertise and networks which offer high value.
- Be open and transparent. This means grantees need to be honest and share the bad news and challenges, instead of just selling good news.
- Streamline and simplify reporting. Avoid custom reports. This is possible where there is trust, a good relationship and

---

[*] Faella, S. & Roberson, R. (2024). The Strategic Value of Trust-Based Philanthropy, Stanford Social Innovation Review. https://doi.org/10.48558/PJXF-V718. This offers examples of trust-based philanthropy and a brief discussion of its merits.
[†] https://www.trustbasedphilanthropy.org/ Many descriptions of trust-based philanthropy exist: this is fairly typical.

openness and transparency. High-reporting requirements are a sign of low trust.

- Multi-year grants so that grantees can plan and invest to deal with long-term problems.

MacKenzie Scott is a leading example of this approach. She has given away over $16 billion to more than 2,000 NGOs in unrestricted funding since 2019,[*] often at a scale which is transformational for the grantee. The long-term effectiveness is not yet known, not least because Scott does not require the impact reporting which most funders demand. She does not even specify when the funds need to be spent; she trusts her grantees to make best use of them. Critics argue that this hides huge waste and that the funds are often 'too large' relative to the size of the grantee.

Scott's trust-based philanthropy is having predictable and positive results. The Centre for Effective Philanthropy reports that 79 per cent of grantees have been able to innovate, introduce new programmes or improve existing programmes; 95 per cent report that their financial capacity has improved and a majority have been able to invest in building their organizational capacity, such as IT, staffing, HR and financial management.[†] These are all outcomes which do not usually happen with restricted funding.

Scott's approach is being mirrored by Melinda French Gates through the Pivotal Foundation.[‡] In 2024 she gave $20 million each to 12 individuals to distribute as they see fit. That was a huge exercise in trust which few other grant funders would countenance. And increasingly, her other grants are not restricted. Again, she prefers to

[*]Philanthropy.com. Sneha Dave, 7 May 2024.
[†]Centre for Effective Philanthropy. Emerging Impacts: The Effects of Mackenzie Scott's Large, Unrestricted Gifts. Results from Year Two of a Three-Year Study. Ellie Buteau, Ph.D., Elisha Smith Arrillaga, Ph.D. and Christina Im.
[‡]Opinion piece by Melinda French Gates in The New York Times, 28 May 2024. https://www.nytimes.com/2024/05/28/opinion/melinda-french-gates-reproductive-rights.html

trust the charities she backs. Arguably, if you do not trust a charity enough to give unrestricted funding, you should not give at all.

Trust-based philanthropy means that grantees have to raise their game and change their game. Charities need to stop treating funders as piggy banks and start treating them as partners, which is what they are. Both the funders and the funded share a common objective and bring different capabilities to the table. The funded often explain in great detail what capabilities they bring, but then they never ask what capabilities the funder brings to the table. Funders bring much more than money to the table. As funders, they will have very wide experience of what does and does not work. They will have seen successes; even more importantly, they will have seen failures. The collective knowledge, wisdom and experience of your funders is like gold dust. They can point in the right direction and help you avoid making some of the biggest mistakes they see elsewhere.

TREATING FUNDERS AS PARTNERS

STIR Education knew that what it was doing was original and untested. It would take years of development to create a solution which was scalable, replicable and sustainable. The question was how to deal with the many funders who all wanted to see results, and see them now.

After much agonizing we did something radical. We decided to treat our funders not as piggy banks, but as partners. To start the partnership, we invited all our funders from around the world to a workshop, to help us design the next phase of our strategy. We set two clear ground rules:

- There would be 100 per cent transparency: funders would see our disasters as well as our triumphs. That is the only way you can build trust and get relevant advice.
- There would be no ask for any money from anyone: this was to focus 100 per cent on tapping into the massive experience and

---

knowledge which our funders had. We knew that with the right advice, they could save us years of wasted development time.

This was highly risky. If it went wrong, we would not lose one funder, we would lose them all and we would be out of business. But we also knew that continuing with the traditional contractual, and slightly adversarial, way of doing business with funders was a waste of their knowledge. We need partnerships, not just contracts.

TESTING THE PARTNERSHIP PRINCIPLE

We were due to fly to New York for the United Nations General Assembly (UNGA). On the Friday, we heard that we had fallen victim to a major fraud in Uganda. What would you do, knowing that on Monday you would start meeting all your major funders on the fringes of UNGA?

First, we sent the COO down to Uganda on the overnight flight to find out what was going on: establish how much damage had been done, what caused the fraud and how it could be contained. Then we went to UNGA. We had a short debate about what to tell our funders. One argument was to stabilize the situation, get a report back from our COO and then tell our funders: telling them about the problem before we had the solution would look amateurish and not inspire confidence. But that would mean not telling them anything on Monday and that would be a huge breach of trust. Trust is the essence of any partnership: if you want to have a partnership, you have to show you can be trusted. So we decided to tell them everything we knew on Monday morning, even though it was still a fast-developing situation. The funders showed a uniform reaction. First, they asked us about what was going on. Then they looked surprised. They were not surprised about a fraud in Uganda: they had heard that sort of story many times. They were astonished that we were being so prompt and open in our disclosure to them. That signalled to them that we really could be trusted. From there on, the only question they asked was 'how can we help?'

The test of any partnership are the tough times, not the good times. Show you can be trusted in good times and bad, and you will sustain the partnership, regardless of whether it is with funders, government or other NGOs.

Trust-based philanthropy forces funders to become far more proactive. Funders cannot afford to wait and respond to proposals from charities. They need to be far more strategic in their funding. They have two ways of doing this:

Back the charity, not the project. Most funders are fairly reactive: they wait to be approached by charities who then make bids and the funder sorts the deserving from the undeserving. This is reasonable: there is no way in which a funder can find out about every innovative charity around the world. But if they find a charity in which they really believe, they should make it a partnership. Be prepared to offer unrestricted funding to build the capacity of the charity and offer it help and advice so that it can fulfil its mission properly. If you really believe in the mission and the charity, that is the best way to make it more effective. If you only slightly trust it and only slightly believe in its mission, then restricting funding is a slightly good way of dealing with your slight belief. The better way of dealing with such doubt is not to fund the charity at all. Have courage to back your beliefs and back the charity, or back out.

Back the mission and then find the right partner charities. If you are deeply committed to a mission, you will know that you cannot do it all yourself. It makes more sense to work with other funders in the same space. Together, you can multiply your convening power and financial power. You can then use this power to bring charities, governments and stakeholders together to find a common solution, or to test and develop innovative approaches. You can move from backing piecemeal initiatives to creating systemic solutions. With the benefit of scale, you can fund multiple pilots and test markets, which will in turn accelerate learning and knowledge acquisition.

In a world where cash is king (or queen), funders have the chance to make the rules. This is the time for them to change the rules.

PRIVATE SECTOR

Many NGOs treat private sector corporates as slightly grubby donors who want to whitewash their profits. This is a mistake, for two reasons:

- The corporate sector can be highly effective donors and supporters
- Corporates can offer scale solutions which NGOs cannot.

The corporate sector can be highly effective donors and supporters
Charities follow the economist Adam Smith in mistrusting the private sector: 'It is not from the benevolence of the butcher, the brewer, or the baker, that we expect our dinner, but from their regard to their own interest.'* But if you can understand the self-interest of a firm, often you can forge a productive relationship with them. The best firms understand that the profit motive requires doing more than simply maximizing revenues and minimizing expenses. For instance, firms need to:

- Demonstrate to regulators, stakeholders and pressure groups that they have a sound ESG (Environmental, Social and Governance) agenda.
- Engage staff: volunteering increases engagement and retention, builds soft skills[†] and improves mental health[‡] and recruitment.
- Have a licence to operate: if you are engaged in alcohol, tobacco, fossil fuels or gambling, you will usually need to

---

An Inquiry into the Nature and Causes of the Wealth of Nations, Adam Smith. Published 1776 by W. Strahan and T. Cadell.
[†]https://www.unitedhealthgroup.com/newsroom/2017/0914studydoinggoodisgoodforyou.html
[‡]Helping people, changing lives: 3 health benefits of volunteering. Angela Thorenson, Mayo Clinic Health System.

demonstrate that you will be a responsible operator and a strong CSR (Corporate Social Responsibility) agenda will be part of that. For instance, when San Miguel was setting up some new breweries in the Philippines,* it had to develop a source of safe, clean water: as part of its agreement with the local government, it became a provider not only of beer, but also of clean water to the community. San Miguel's self-interest was also in the public interest.

- Meet government CSR regulations: in India, corporates are required to give 2 per cent of their profits to charitable causes, for instance.

All of this means that many firms want to work with relevant NGOs, but you have to remember Adam Smith and understand 'their own self-interest'. As with grants officers of foundations, the grants officers in firms face pressures which you have to respect:

- They have to show that grants are aligned to the mission and interests of the firm: CSR funds are always under pressure. They must show their relevance and impact each year. Given unpredictable profit cycles, CSR funds are often not known far in advance: be patient and build a long-term relationship so that you can move fast when you need to.
- Grants have to be aligned with their CSR strategy. If volunteering is a large part of their agenda, consider how you can use them. It is difficult to use 100 people for a day as part of their annual conference. But you may well be able to use the skills of a senior executive on your board to support your HR, finance or PR teams. Corporate skills can be as valuable as corporate money. Getting the right HR or legal advice at the start of a tricky issue can save a fortune in time and money later.

*The author was working with San Miguel in the Philippines during this period.

138

Once you have a relationship with a firm, you will usually find there are many ways they can help which go well beyond money and board skills. A few examples will make the point:

- McKinsey & Company let Teach First use their offices to meet key stakeholders and potential recruits when it started up. Immediately, all the awkward questions about the credibility of the startup team vanished.
- A&O Shearman* allow Coachbright to use its offices for board meetings, saving significant costs on having to hire a room.
- Rothschild & Co. hosted a breakfast for Right to Succeed: this had significant convening power with policy makers and key influencers.

These are low-cost but high-impact interventions for firms to offer small NGOs.

Corporates can offer scale solutions that NGOs cannot
The private sector often has one thing which charities struggle with: access to the people you want to serve. The private sector can afford to invest in acquiring customers, building infrastructure and setting up an effective supply chain. If you can tap into the resources of the private sector, you can achieve scale and scope which would be impossible for you to achieve alone.

DISCOVERING THE POWER OF THE PRIVATE SECTOR

Although I arrived jet-lagged at the airport in Port Moresby, my baggage did not arrive and it may or may not have been jet-lagged. Air France had lost my baggage, again. Fortunately, this was a predictable event, so I had all my valuable possessions with me as

---

*A&O Shearman was known as Allen & Overy until June 2024.

hand baggage. All I lacked was anything to wear, beyond what I was already wearing.

Port Moresby is possibly the only international airport to have a second-hand clothes shop in arrivals. I went there and kitted myself out in clothes which had clearly been donated in charity drives in America. I left the shop wearing a T-shirt proudly projecting the logo of the Tijuana Rock Festival, with a large picture of a cannabis plant on the front.

At first it seemed outrageous that traders were profiting from the generosity of donors in Tijuana and elsewhere. But it soon made sense. At markets all over Papua New Guinea, I saw stalls hawking similar second-hand clothes. The traders were solving a problem for the donors: how could they get the right clothes to the right people at low cost?

The traders knew what sort of clothes people wanted to buy. They selected the right clothes, transported them at very low cost into the distant highlands and then made them available at affordable prices. The market was doing what any centrally planned system or charity would struggle to do: it was allocating scarce resource efficiently and economically.

The profit and not-for-profit sectors worked together to find an effective solution, and I got something to wear. Everyone was a winner.

We have already noted how Imazon has become the trusted partner to governments in tackling deforestation. Imazon does this by being a neutral and reliable source of information on deforestation, which it accesses largely from satellite data in near real time. Despite having a small budget of just $5 million a year, it is now raising its game. In 2015 it created MapBiomas, which maps all nine of Brazil's biomes and tracks changes since 1985. This is a vast data exercise. It is able to do this because it has a partnership with Google: Imazon's algorithms combine with Google's computing power and satellite imagery to create a powerful service.

WSUP (Water and Sanitation for the Urban Poor) is a good example of how working with the private sector can sometimes be the only way to deliver a solution. Their challenge is encapsulated in their name: how can you provide water and sanitation to the urban poor?[*] Many of these people live in informal settlements or slums where the only toilets are flying toilets: waste is bagged and thrown away. Even where there are toilets, there is no way of emptying them. From the outset, WSUP recognized that 'water doesn't just come out of a tap, it flows from a functioning system – not just made up of boreholes and pipes, but of the people, institutions, regulators, businesses, and politicians who manage it.'[†] This means they do not just bore wells, but they seek system solutions with the public and private sectors.

In 2015 WSUP developed a partnership in Bangladesh called SWEEP which enabled small-scale operators to lease vacuum tankers from the public sector in four cities. These operators are able to offer low-cost services to low-income households. This dramatically expanded the number of operators and improved sanitation in places where there was no mains drainage. It was a classic, profit-driven win for everyone: for the small-scale operators, for the low-income households, for the government and for the sanitation board.

Similarly, Grameen realized that although it could address the challenge of poverty directly through micro-finance, it could not address the challenge of poor nutrition. Grameen lacked the expertise in food production, safety and distribution. Grameen teamed up with Danone[‡] following a meeting between Muhammad Yunus and

---

[*] Scaling Pathways: The Water and Sanitation for the Urban Poor Story, March 2019.
[†] https://wsup.com/about-us/what-we-do/ Retrieved 8 June 2024.
[‡] Yunus, Muhammad (2007). *Creating a World Without Poverty*. New York: Public Affairs (ISBN 978-1586484934).

Franck Riboud, chairman and CEO of Danone in 2005. Danone's R&D arm then worked with another NGO, 'Global Alliance for Improved Nutrition' to develop Shokti+. This is a high-nutrition yoghurt which enables children to get the vitamins, calcium and iron they need. Each end of the supply chain helps alleviate poverty: the milk comes from farmers who may have been financed by Grameen microfinance; the milk is then sold door to door in rural villages by micro-entrepreneurs who may also have been financed by Grameen. In between, Danone produces the yoghurt in safe and sanitary conditions. In urban areas, the yoghurt is sold through Danone's distribution network to stalls and small shops. Grameen uses any profit it makes in the urban areas to subsidize sales in rural areas.

The Grameen–Danone* joint venture has been set up as a social enterprise: any profits are ploughed back into the organization to further its social objectives. As we shall see in the next chapter on 'Money', creating a social enterprise can be a powerful way of ensuring the economic sustainability of your mission. You can put the profit focus to good use. By making your intervention financially self-supporting, you no longer have to worry about the challenges of fund raising and the gyrations of government policy and support.

Instead of seeing profit as the problem, see profit as the solution. Profit enables you to build a self-sustaining solution to a social challenge; it also motivates private sector partners to work with you in a meaningful way. It is nice when they lend you some office space or hold a reception for you, but you benefit most when you can use their technical know-how, access to customers and supply chain. You will do that when you can show that they will benefit economically from your idea.

*https://www.danonecommunities.com/grameen-danone-foods-ltd/

OTHER NGOS

Partnerships with other NGOs are even more difficult than partnerships with the private sector because:

- There is no rational basis for resource allocation. Instead of the profit motive, two parties have to argue about how best to achieve a mission and they will have different missions: it is a recipe for conflict, not collaboration.
- Resource scarcity means that the battle for resource allocation is even greater than in the private sector.
- Governance is always a challenge: neither party wants to be the minor player. Most charities know the pain of being a sub-contractor and want to avoid it, but a partnership of equals can be very unstable.

Most NGO partnerships are not driven by altruism or belief in the mission, they are driven by money. In practice, cash is king: if you have the contract and the money, then you can dictate terms. This recreates all the challenges of sub-contracting with the private sector which we explored previously.

At the heart of any successful NGO partnership you will need:

- Clear goals: how success will be measured for each player, and there should be wins for everyone;
- Clear roles: who does what;
- Clear governance: how decisions get made.

This can be achieved without the traditional buyer/vendor relationship. The role of the lead NGO should be to create the framework in which everyone can succeed, not just the lead contractor. This has been the approach of Right to Succeed (RtS),* which improves

---

*The author was chair of Right to Succeed during this period.

education systems across a local area. RtS recognizes that this needs to be a community-wide effort, not an effort for the glorification of RtS. That means it puts in place a governance structure which reflects the interests of all the key stakeholders including local schools and local government. This creates a more objective decision-making process which generates commitment and buy-in. But to do this, RtS has to be very clear about where it can and cannot add value. Ultimately, it adds value in four ways:

- Diagnosing the challenge and capability to change
- Building a coalition for change
- Creating a change management framework and process
- Putting in rigorous measurement and evaluation processes.

This framework allows other specialist NGOs to focus on delivering their particular special skill, which might be for instance: literacy, numeracy, dealing with special needs children, parental and community engagement. In ten years it has had to learn the hard way how to do this. It sounds easy, but it is not: dictating terms is always easier than real collaboration. Ultimately, real collaboration leads to better and more sustainable results.

Although NGO partnerships are hard, they are not impossible. An extreme form of partnership was a three-way initiative between the British Council, Voluntary Service Overseas (VSO) and Education Development Trust (EDT). As ever, it was the client imperative which forced them to find an innovative solution: they realized that they would never succeed working against each other, so they had to both bid and implement as one. They did this by creating a virtual merger of the three organizations for the duration of the project (see box below). This ensured that everyone on the project was working for the same team with the same goals.

CREATING A VIRTUAL MERGER*

A virtual merger is a halfway house between a partnership and a formal merger. It was a highly innovative solution created to support the government of Rwanda's education reforms. Delivering on the government's agenda was beyond the capacity of any single NGO so three NGOs came together to form a virtual merger. They created a special purpose vehicle designed solely to deliver the Rwanda government's agenda around primary school language education. The three organizations were Voluntary Service Overseas (VSO), the British Council and Education Development Trust (EDT); the project was funded by the UK government through its aid agency, DfID. This was a potential nightmare of five different stakeholders all attempting to collaborate.

The three NGOs quickly realized that working separately would be a recipe for chaos so they pooled their efforts and staff into one temporary organization called Building Learning Foundations (BLF). This integration was so strong that going into their office in Kigali, the only signage anywhere was for Building Learning Foundations: there was no signage from any of the three NGOs behind the alliance. It was impossible to tell which staff came from which organization. They had all been seconded full time to BLF, so their interest was in the success of BLF, not of their parent organization.

Governance was helped by the discipline of the Rwanda Government. Every town mayor has to sign a performance contract, which is reviewed by the President: if the mayor fails to deliver, the mayor is removed. BLF was part of their performance

---

*The author was international chair of EDT at the time. This case is based on a field visit to Rwanda.

contract, so they were highly committed to making sure it worked.

This virtual merger was a deep partnership. It worked because all the stakeholders shared the same goals: they all needed the project to succeed. Differences between organizations were largely eliminated by having a common governance structure and a common branding: there was little sense of 'us' and 'them'.

The virtual merger shows that you can be creative about how you achieve scale to deliver your mission. But virtual mergers, like all partnerships, require well-aligned goals, common incentives and strong governance. Success or failure is assured before you start: set the merger up for success or walk away.

As with all partnerships, it is easy to be enthusiastic at the start when there are opportunities to be chased, but that is exactly the time you need to start asking the awkward questions. If all you ask is 'how will we succeed?', you will fail to deal with the more important questions: 'what might go wrong and how will we deal with it?' Use the good times to build trust, build understanding and prepare for the bad times.

PARTNERSHIPS: SUMMARY

Partnerships are powerful and perilous in equal proportion. They are powerful because they let you achieve impact without having to scale your organization to unsustainable levels. Partnerships help in four ways:

- Scaling
- Scope
- Funding
- Learning.

These partnerships can be with:

- Government, who can ensure maximum scale at speed, but are often hard to work with and may be unreliable.
- Funders, who offer not just money but a wealth of experience about what works.
- Private sector, which can offer expertise, facilities, low-cost distribution, technology and sustainable economic models that allow your mission to succeed.
- Other NGOs, who can help broaden the scope of your intervention to provide a comprehensive solution to the challenge at hand.

The perils of these partnerships are the four Cs: creep, control, complexity and capacity.

- Creep: cash is king and it is very easy to follow the cash. That results in following the needs of your funder and may mean losing sight of your mission.
- Control: the stronger your partner, the less control you have.
- Complexity: serving the reporting requirements of one donor can be onerous. Serving 20 different donors all with different programmes and different reporting requirements means that you will drown in complexity.
- Capacity: funders hate to fund 'overhead', but if you have no investment in HR, IT, training, learning and development you become hollowed out. You need to build capacity to succeed.

Decide what sort of relationships you want with all your stakeholders: are they purely contractual, or are they real partnerships based on mutual trust, support and shared interests? Partnerships are hard to build but have high value.

5

Money

Find it, manage it and make the most of it

Founders of charities tend to have a love–hate relationship with money. They love the money, but hate having to find it. They want to focus on their idea, not on the money. But you cannot change the world without money, so you need a clear plan for finding and using money to best effect.

This chapter will show:

- *Why money makes running an NGO far harder than running a for-profit business*
- *How to cross the startup hurdle with nearly no money*
- *How to build and rebuild your business plan*
- *How to avoid the seven deadly sins of money.*

WHY MONEY MAKES RUNNING AN NGO FAR HARDER THAN RUNNING A FOR-PROFIT BUSINESS

People in the for-profit sector often make the lazy assumption that working in the not-for-profit sector must be an easy option for second-rate managers. They assume that the iron discipline of profit focus forces managers to up their game, especially in competitive markets. Anyone who has worked in both sectors will vouch that working in the not-for-profit sector is far harder than in the for-profit sector. Here are five reasons why managing an NGO is so tough:

Lack of profit focus does not make things easier, it makes things harder. Profit focus means decision making is relatively easy: decisions can be reduced to a calculation of Net Present Value (NPV) or Internal Rate of Return (IRR) or other measures of return on investment (ROI). There will be arguments over these calculations and the trade-offs they represent, but at least the focus and the rules of the game are clear.

In the not-for-profit sector, there is no simple metric around which to base decisions on how to use your budget, how much budget is required and how to prioritize resources usage. Focus on the mission is vague: there are many ways in which you can focus on the mission and there are normally many ways in which the mission can be interpreted. Worse, focus on the mission invariably means that spending which is not mission critical gets ignored. The result is that finance, IT, training and research are under-funded, which damages the long-term health of the organization.

Scale is a problem, not a benefit. In the private sector, scale is usually a big benefit. With scale, you can reduce unit costs; increase your advertising and research, improve your market position, make more profit and beat the competition. In the not-for-profit sector, more scale often leads to more problems. When you start up, it is relatively easy to find a few funders to support your modest financial needs. Finding $100,000 is fairly easy; finding $10 million or $100 million of funding every year becomes harder and harder. The larger you become, the faster the fundraising treadmill spins. You have to run faster and faster just to stay still. Not-for-profits have to find creative solutions to the problem of scale.

There are few economies of scale in the not-for-profit sector. In many cases, there are diseconomies of scale. At startup, a charity will often put in a huge amount of sweat equity and tender loving care to make the proof of concept work. This is not a scalable proposition. As you grow, you have to build a machine to deliver; you can no longer take shortcuts on financial reporting, controls or regulatory compliance and you will need to invest in IT and other infrastructure. Most charities depend on human contact to deliver their services: it is hard to find scale economies in human contact. Once again, charities have to be highly creative if they are to find scale economies. As we have seen in previous chapters, this often comes through partnerships and through reducing and focusing activities onto a critical core.

Lack of resources. Every private sector firm likes to believe that they have a lean operation. To test that assumption, try walking into the offices of a charity, then walk into the offices of one of the charity's corporate funders. The corporate office will be a palace compared to the hovel of the charity. If the private sector is lean, the charity sector is emaciated. This is a real challenge for management. It means that you cannot buy your way out of trouble. You cannot quietly pay off a disruptive employee, nor can you afford the cost of an employment tribunal: you have to get hiring and firing 100 per cent right. You will not be able to afford consultants to help you make the right decisions and avoid mistakes: you have to get it right yourself. Neither can you afford to get into legal disputes, because you cannot afford the legal costs: you have to get all your contracts right yourself. Lack of resources means that you have no room for error. NGO management is management on the high wire, without a safety net.

Lack of capital. Most charities operate with three to six months of reserves: if they fail to raise money or cut costs, they will be out of business in three to six months. In addition, they rarely have anything very much in the way of tangible assets, such as buildings, plant or equipment. This makes it very hard to borrow money, because they cannot offer any collateral for a loan. And they do not have the option of raising money through equity financing, as they have no equity. All of this makes it very hard for charities to invest in the future, through research or testing innovative ideas. It also makes it hard for them to take on contracts with a long payback: charities are in a constant struggle for cash flow.

The implications of these challenges are:

- Strong day-to-day financial management to manage cash flow is essential.

151

- Charities have to focus on their magic sauce: be very clear about where they add most value and strip away all other activities.
- A clear business model is vital: match your theory of change to the resources available. This is a process of discovery over time, so you need to keep on flexing your business model.
- There is a market failure in terms of helping charities take on longer-term projects where the payback may be delayed. This market failure is being addressed by various initiatives such as PBR, SIB and more, which are explained later in this chapter.
- Strong management is non-optional. Charities need the best, not the second-best, talent in the market.
- Good governance is required to ensure that these challenges are addressed properly.

Never believe that running a charity is the easy option.

HOW TO CROSS THE STARTUP HURDLE WITH NEARLY NO MONEY
The good news is that you do not need a lot of money to start up:

- Muhammad Yunus started Grameen Bank by lending just $27 of his own money.
- Teach First started with a cup of tea and a long conversation between two people. It is now the largest graduate recruiter in the UK.
- STIR started with an investment of £3,000, which was probably £2,000 too much. It now supports the education of 6 million children globally.

The even better news is that you do not need to put your own money at risk, unless it is pocket money which you can afford to lose like Yunus and his first lending to villagers in Bangladesh. In practice, you should not put your own savings at risk in support of your idea. You will believe in your idea and will probably become passionate about it. That means you are likely to be blind to its risks and limitations. Do not invest in a flawed idea, especially if it is your idea. You should build your charity with other people's money only. If you cannot raise any money from anyone that says one of three things:

- No one believes in your idea, in which case you need to adapt it.
- No one believes in you, in which case you need to find some credible partners to work with you.
- Your idea is good, but your pitch is flawed, in which case you need to adapt your pitch.

In any event, market testing your idea is the best way to discover whether your idea is going to succeed or not. The market gives brutal but valuable feedback to you.

Despite this good news, you need to find some way of going from idea to action and the bridge you have to cross is made of money. Your priorities should be:

- Build your business case
- Sell your business case
- Test lean.

Build your business case. The substance of your business case is covered in the next section. At startup, you will not be able to produce a full or credible business plan. You will have an idea, but it is highly unlikely that you will have either the skills or the knowledge to build a complete business plan. In the cases above:

- Yunus was a professor at a university, not a banker: he had neither the knowledge nor the expertise to build the business case for a bank.

- Teach First was started by two people with no experience of education in the UK, so we had no idea what the practical implications of our idea would be or how much the idea would cost.
- STIR focuses on building intrinsic motivation from minister to child across education systems. There was no one on earth who knew either how to do that or how much it might cost.

Know what you do not know: recognize that you do not have the knowledge or expertise to build your business plan. Instead, reach out to people who do have expertise and knowledge. Each expert may only hold one piece of the jigsaw puzzle: your job is to integrate all the insights and inputs into a coherent plan. For instance, in starting Teach First different experts were able to tell us how much training teachers would cost, how much it might cost to recruit graduates, how much selection would cost, how much in school support would cost and how much we might have to invest in technology, finance and support functions. None of the experts could see the full picture, but each one had credible knowledge in their own area.

By building your business case with experts you achieve four goals at the same time:

- You receive valuable feedback on the viability of your idea and you can improve it based on that feedback.
- You identify potential supporters and backers: asking for advice is a soft, easy and highly effective form of engagement. People are flattered to be asked for their advice and having given their advice they are more emotionally committed to the success of your idea, because they start to think that it is *their* idea.
- You build the credibility of your business case. When funders quiz you on your business case they may find it hard to know if your numbers are credible or not. But if you can say that your numbers have been validated by an expert in

each field, the credibility of your business case will be greatly enhanced.

- You minimize your personal risk. These conversations let you assess the viability of your idea. By the time you finish, you will know if you have a viable proposition on your hands or not.

The process of building a business case is highly iterative. You may change not only your business model, but your entire idea. For instance, in the for-profit sector I decided to start a bank. This requires over $1 billion of capital, which I never have had and never will. The initial idea was for an internet-based retail bank; by the time the funding was approved it had become a mixed internet and physical bank focused on firms with $10 to $100 million turnover. There would be no retail offer. It was completely different from the original idea.

You will receive critical feedback on your idea, which may be constructive or not. It is easy to react emotionally: critical feedback can feel like an attack on you, not on your idea. Don't take it personally. All feedback is useful, so use it: improve your plan in response to every piece of feedback you receive.

Sell your business case. When you start out, you will not have a business case. You will just have an idea. That is all you need at the start. Initially, you are not testing the financial viability of your idea, but the market viability of it:

- Does the idea fill a real need?
- Is there anyone else already doing this?
- How will this idea be different or better than other ideas out there?

At startup, you need stamina, not money. You can discuss your idea with key stakeholders while you still have your day job. There is no need to risk your day job until you have gained in principle support from key backers.

155

As you discuss your idea with experts, potential backers and other stakeholders, you can slowly start to build your business plan. Building your business plan and selling your business plan go hand in hand.

At the heart of selling your plan is the validation process. This is where you get different experts to validate different elements of your plan. Never ask them to validate the whole plan, because that gives them the chance to express unhelpful opinions on subjects they know nothing about. Simply get each person to validate that the element of the plan as it relates to them is accurate and acceptable. You then need to assemble each piece of the jigsaw into an operational plan and financial plan for formal approval. When challenged on any element of the plan, you should be able to refer back to experts or stakeholders who have validated that part of the plan.

SELLING TEACH FIRST

Selling your business plan is not just an intellectual exercise, it is about building a coalition of success. And your business plan is not just about numbers, it is about a coherent operational plan which sits behind the numbers. As you sell your idea, you will constantly refine and improve your plan in response to each stakeholder who must validate different parts of your plan, as we found out with Teach First:

- Businesses: to agree that they support the concept and would give preferential recruitment treatment to graduates of the Teach First programme. This was vital for the on-campus value proposition about leadership: it showed that joining Teach First opened up career opportunities rather than closing them down.
- Teacher Development Agency (TDA) was responsible for teacher recruitment. They agreed that there was a recruitment challenge, that we would fill a gap in the market which they

---

could not cover. We would not be duplicating effort and wasting tax payer money.

- Initial Teacher Training (ITT) providers had to confirm that they believed it would be possible to train teachers in six weeks, not the traditional two years, provided that they were given enough in school support.
- Funders needed to agree that they would fund the elements of the programme which government could not fund, such as the initial recruitment and selection, charity overhead and the leadership training programme.
- Unions agreed that our teachers would be working on the right terms and conditions, consistent with their policies and expectations.
- Universities had to let us recruit on campus and give us support in their placement offices.
- Head teachers and their unions agreed that they would accept the teachers into their schools.
- McKinsey & Company provided a study to show that there were enough graduates who we could target to make the programme viable.
- Officials and advisors at the Department for Education helped steer the programme in the right direction to make sure that it was politically acceptable.

As we validated our business plan with each of these stakeholders, we had to flex and adapt our original idea. In doing so, we painstakingly built a coalition of willing supporters. All of this had to be done before we approached the minister for formal approval. He promptly chucked the idea, and us, out of his office. We returned a month later with a revised plan and he approved it. You need stamina to build a coalition, not money.

The validation and selling process is time consuming. You should probably estimate the size of the job before you set out, simply so that you can set your own expectations of how long it will take and how much time you need to invest. Using the Teach First example again, we needed:

- Number of stakeholders involved: over 50.
- Number of meetings per stakeholder: at least two for most of them, nearer ten for the top ten stakeholders.
- Number of calls needed to fix each meeting: two or three, plus follow-up time writing notes, confirming outcomes and agreeing next steps.

That meant we made well over 500 stakeholder calls before we even began to get started. Each time the questions would be the same, assuming that we had managed to find the right person and navigate our way past reception, secretaries and various dragons and beasts that always protect important people from unimportant people:

- 'who are you (do I know you and do I care to speak to you)?'
- 'who do you represent (are you important enough)?'
- 'what do you want (why should I bother talking to you)?'
- 'I will see if my PA can organize something (preferably in the next century)'

As an unknown startup with no relevant expertise, these are very hard questions to answer. The reality is that you have to blag: you have to talk yourself up to get noticed. You will find that as an individual, you have little credibility unless you are already well known in your field. You have to borrow credibility from wherever you can. Talk up any contacts you have had with anyone or anything. Even a short conversation with a power broker can help: 'I am following up on a discussion with Mrs Big Shot of Mega Corp.' Be careful not to misrepresent: the chances are that your key stakeholders all talk to each other but you can put a positive spin on whatever contact you have had.

The first conversations are the hardest: you do not know your topic and you do not know the stakeholders. After the first few meetings, things get easier. You start to master your topic and avoid novice errors. You begin to build a network, which becomes self-reinforcing. Always ask one stakeholder to introduce you to another, because a warm introduction is 10 times easier than a cold call. As you meet more people, you build your credibility and you can build momentum.

Selling should be very low cost. The main cost is to you and your time. You may also need to spend a little on travel. Although video conferencing is good, it is far better to meet people face to face when you meet them for the first time. That is how you can build rapport. Once you have a relationship and basis of trust, you can use video calling.

Perhaps the only area where you might want to spend a little money is on a domain name, website and email address. You can also set up an Instagram page and other social media sites. All of this can be done at very low cost. Professional freelancers can often produce a polished appearance for you for a modest outlay. This is purely defensive spending. You are not going to sell your business plan on the basis of a website and social media but anyone you meet for the first time will want to check you out online. If you have a professional-looking website, that will give them some assurance. Also make sure that your personal online profile is appropriate and up to date: this is not the time to record your antics at a drunken stag or hen party.

Selling your business plan is hard work, but it can be managed in your spare or discretionary time. This is also when you define the future success of your venture. As all generals know, most battles are won or lost before the first shot is fired. Discover whether you are likely to win or lose before you engage in the battle of delivering the mission and building your organization.

Test lean. The best way to evaluate your idea is to test it in the market place. Experts do not get everything right all the time: experts built the

Titanic and an amateur built the Ark. The best proof you will ever bring to funders and stakeholders is a proof of concept: a test which has worked. At this stage you need to be both creative and realistic.

Be creative. You can't spend money you do not have so find ways of testing your idea without spending. For a start, you will not need all the overhead of an established charity. You do not need to spend anything on offices or infrastructure. You should be able to find a few willing helpers to volunteer their time.

STARTING UP START UP

Start Up for ex-offenders helped prisoners start up their own legitimate businesses on release from prison. Testing the idea was vital, because there were no experts to help build the business plan. It was an idea which had never been tried before, so no one knew if it would work or not. The only way to discover if it would work was to test it in practice.

Testing required gaining access to prisons and prisoners. This was made possible because:

- Juliet Hope, the founder, is a force of nature and it is hard to say no to her: this is the classic symptom of a great social entrepreneur. The best social entrepreneurs do not understand the words 'no' or 'impossible' and have an unlimited well of energy and enthusiasm for their idea.
- Prison governors are desperate for anything that might help them on the inside and help reduce their customer base. They are one of the few professions that want fewer customers but given they have virtually no discretionary budget, they favour free initiatives: Juliet offered a free initiative.
- Most prisons have an existing business programme: this gave both the governors and the charity a vehicle to use. It also gave

---

the charity a way of working with and vetting potential startup candidates.

Juliet then twisted arms to persuade volunteers to help with the programme on the inside and to provide mentoring to the ex-offenders on the outside. She persuaded a bank to offer banking services to the ex-offenders and an insurance company to provide insurance cover: normally ex-offenders find it very hard to access these services. With all this voluntary help, the core of the programme was in place and ready to test.

Eventually, they found that the only investment required was a modest startup grant to help each business get going: this was often a matter of buying tools for the job for the ex-offender. Each ex-offender receives a discharge payment of £89.52,* which is meant to cover them for six weeks until they start receiving benefits. The chances of them finding enough money to buy the tools for their trade are about the same as winning the lottery.

Testing the business was very low cost because the major inputs (time and effort) were all free.

Start Up could not prove in theory that it would work. It could only prove it would work by testing the idea and then adapting it based on experience. Instead of the business following the business plan, the business plan had to follow the business: test, then plan instead of plan, then test.

Testing lean is vital, not just because that is probably all you can afford. Testing fat is unscalable. Some new charities are so keen to prove the viability of their idea that they throw huge amounts of resource into the proof of concept. The actual money spent may be low, but the amount of effort may be very high, often given by deeply committed volunteers who go above and beyond the call of duty to

*Prison discharge policy: PSI 72/2011 HM Prison and Probation Service, 16 August 2023.

make the idea work. This ensures that the proof of concept works: if you throw enough time and passion at any idea, you can normally make it work. But it is a completely unscalable model. You cannot scale vast amounts of voluntary and passionate commitment.

HOW TO AVOID THE SEVEN DEADLY SINS OF MONEY

For-profit entrepreneurs are very focused on money. They may succeed or fail, but it is not for lack of interest or focus on money. Social entrepreneurs are different. They are interested in their idea, not in making money. This means many social entrepreneurs are naive about money and it can often be their downfall.

From bitter experience, here are seven of the most common money mistakes social entrepreneurs make. Just by knowing these mistakes, you give yourself a chance of avoiding them. You may make your own money mistakes, but at least they will be original and hopefully, they will not be fatal:

1. Underselling your idea
2. Weak controls
3. Accounting conventions
4. Optimism and denial
5. Dependency
6. Unsustainability
7. Underinvestment.

1. Underselling your idea

Underselling takes two forms: scale and frequency.

Scale underselling is when you do not ask for enough money or resource. This is a classic sign of someone who does not really believe in their idea. It is a good way to undermine your own credibility. If you claim you are going to change the world in five years and you only need $10,000, you will not be believed. Be clear about what you need. This will force you to speak to the right funders.

For instance, STIR Education started with a small pilot, which required about $300,000 in funding. We could speak to funders who were prepared to risk small amounts on a new idea: receiving $20,000 would be a very good outcome from a meeting. These startup donors were brilliant because they made a risky bet on an unproven idea but they did not have the capacity to take the idea to scale. As the scale of the challenge became clear, we had to change focus. We realized we would need about $15 million over five years. That forced STIR to talk to different sorts of funders who could raise large amounts of money.

Be confident in your idea and be realistic about what it will take to deliver it.

Frequency underselling is when you simply do not go out and speak to enough funders. This is a natural error to make, because these can be difficult discussions. Raising money is always less interesting than delivering the programme. Failing to sell often enough leads to three problems:

- Reliance on a few funders, which is highly risky.
- Weak sales funnel leading to the risk of having to restructure and reduced programmes and costs.
- Inability to attract new funders, leading to a cliff edge when existing funders' terms expire.

2. Weak controls

Never assume that bad stuff is what happens to other people. You cannot tell what sort of bad stuff will happen, when it will happen or who will cause it. But it will happen, either as a result of incompetence or malfeasance. Strong financial, compliance and governance controls are your defence against the bad stuff. This runs counter to the instincts of many social entrepreneurs who want to focus on the programme: they get turned off by the costs and bureaucracy of control systems. They only discover the value of controls when their absence leads to losses and a crisis. But prevention is better than cure. Typical examples of where controls make a difference:

- Malfeasance: fraud prevention
- Incompetence: over spending on budgets, unauthorized spending and inappropriate contractual commitments.

Typically, the main control system at startup is called trust. This works, more or less, when you have a very small team who all know each other and trust each other. But it is not a scalable system. As you grow, you need to improve your control environment continually. Typically, social enterprises build their control environment too slowly and it is always playing catch-up with the reality on the ground. Invest in controls early and you avoid crisis later. The key controls include:

- Scheme of delegation: who can approve what. Normally, larger transactions require more signatories and more senior signatories. This scheme of delegation will change as the organization and budgets grow.
- Separation of duties: ensure different people enter a transaction and approve it, or negotiate a contract and approve it. It is easy for one person to commit fraud if they control the whole system. It is much harder for fraud to happen when different people have to conspire together for the fraud to work.
- Banking controls: be very clear over who has access to banking systems and who can enter and authorize payments. This is where segregation of duties and your scheme of delegation really matter.
- Monthly reporting cycle: ensure all budget holders report accurately and on time. And check the accuracy of reporting: trust is good, checking is better.

As a social entrepreneur, control environments are probably an alien planet to you and you do not need to become an expert in them. Instead, you need to find the right people to help you. There are three flavours of the 'right people':

- *Accountant or chief financial officer.* Your CFO may well become your right-hand person. A good CFO will be your eyes and ears financially. They will worry about the financial numbers, which frees you up to worry about the programme and managing external stakeholders, including funders.
- *Board, including a finance committee.* A good board and finance committee will make sure you are asking the right questions at the right time and that you have the right control environment for your scale of operation. A poor finance committee just becomes a bureaucratic nightmare which demands and devours ever more paperwork and reports.
- *Auditors.* The annual audit is as welcome and as useful as your bi-annual check-up with the dentist. Your auditors will find out where your controls are weak. This is painful but valuable feedback. Good auditors are constructive: they will understand your situation and make appropriate recommendations on how you can improve.

3. Accounting conventions
Accounting conventions can be really boring for non-accountants – and they often are boring – but they are vital and they exist for good reason. Here are two conventions which trip up many first-time social entrepreneurs:

Restricted versus unrestricted funding. As ever, life in the not-for-profit sector is harder than in the for-profit sector. If a for-profit firm earns some money, it can spend it however it wants to as long as it is legal. If a charity receives some money from a donor, there is a high probability that it will be restricted: you can only use the money for the programme or purpose you have agreed with the funder.

And the funder will expect you to be able to track your spending and prove that you have spent the money as agreed. This not only adds complexity and bureaucracy, it also adds massive risk. You may well find that some programmes are very well funded, while other programmes are underfunded. And you will face a constant struggle to fund your support functions, because funders think that they are a waste of money. At the extreme, your charity can go bust even though it has plenty of money: if all your money is restricted, you may not have money to pay the rent.

Your sacred and serious money comes in the form of unrestricted funding. This is money you can spend at your discretion. It could be for testing new ideas, but is also a vital buffer against disaster. Unrestricted funding can plug gaps in underfunded programmes or if the charity as a whole faces a cash crunch. It is hard to build up unrestricted funds, so avoid using them unless you have to: they are your insurance policy against disaster. Knowing your restricted from your unrestricted funding positions might just save your charity in a crisis.

Cash versus accruals. Social entrepreneurs tend to focus closely on cash, with good reason: if you run out of cash, you run out of business. Month-end payroll has a habit of concentrating the mind. If you can't pay staff, you are in trouble, not in business. Cash focus means that entrepreneurs easily miss the importance of accruals and revenue recognition.

You need to know your position not only today, but also what it will be in the future. For instance, if you have received a large grant, your cash position will look good. This often means that you are now committed to delivering a programme in return for the grant, so you have not only acquired an asset (the cash): you have also acquired a liability (the requirement to deliver a programme). If you recognize all the income immediately, you may be tempted to use it and then you will then run out of money when time comes to deliver the programme. Always understand your future liabilities, not just your current cash position.

Aside from programme commitments and liabilities, you may acquire other liabilities which you do not have to pay for yet. For instance, if you commit to a conference in three months' time you may just pay a 10 per cent deposit now to secure the facilities. Your cash position now looks good, but in three months you have to pay some major bills. You need to be able to accrue for such expenses: recognize them so that you do not get surprised by them later.

As with your control systems, you do not need to be an expert to manage all of this. You need to hire the right people to manage it for you. Your job is to make sure you ask the right questions and you understand what the experts are telling you.

4. Optimism and denial

Social entrepreneurs are natural optimists and enthusiasts. You need to be relentlessly positive: if you are not enthusiastic then no one else will be enthusiastic for you. And there are always plenty of negative people willing to talk you down. Optimism is a real strength, but all strengths become weaknesses when taken to extremes. You are at an extreme when you believe, like Voltaire's Dr Pangloss that 'all is for the best in the best of all possible worlds.'*

When it comes to financial matters, pay heed to the Stockdale paradox,† which holds that true optimism includes an ability to face the brutal facts. It was this version of optimism which helped Admiral Stockdale endure years of harsh treatment as a prisoner of war. You need to face reality and find a way through it. This is especially true of fundraising. The fundraising funnel is a very leaky bucket: it needs replenishing as fast as you leak money out by spending it.

The antidote to optimism and denial is a robust forecasting system: this should take the form of a funding funnel where you can see all your funding prospects, how much you are asking them for, when

---

*Candide, Voltaire, 1759.
†See *Good to Great: Why Some Companies Make the Leap...and Others Don't:* 1 Hardcover – 1 January 2001 by Jim Collins, Harper Business. Note that many of the good to great firms analyzed have gone bust, been taken over or overtaken. Stockdale was a prisoner of war during the Vietnam war. The paradox was that prisoners who hoped to get lucky gave up when their false optimism failed to materialize. Survivors had a different version of optimism which included facing the brutal truth, helping each other and never doubting that you will prevail eventually.

you expect a decision and your likelihood of success. Armed with this, you can estimate how much money you expect to receive and when you expect to receive it. The financial health of your organization is predicted by the health of your funding funnel. The funnel will quickly tell you if you need to take action.

From a governance perspective, when a funding funnel is missing or incomplete that becomes an immediate red flag: it indicates something is wrong and something is being hidden. Good news is rarely hidden from anyone.

5. Dependency

When you find a big funder, it can be like Christmas come early. Suddenly, all your money worries vanish into thin air. You no longer need to take the begging bowl around to countless other funders nor endure repeated rejections because your funder has sorted out your funding challenges. What could possibly go wrong? Well, at least four things can go wrong when you depend too much on one funder:

The funder changes direction. One charity* started in India and was able to scale fast on the back of a grant from DfID (the UK's development agency). DfID was the perfect scaling partner. In addition to money, it brought expertise and networks. The charity rose to the scaling challenge. One year later, DfID announced it would no longer fund programmes in India: its strategic priority had switched to poorer and more fragile states. That was a rational decision which nearly destroyed the charity: DfID represented 80 per cent of its income. Overnight, the charity had to find a way of replacing 80 per cent of its income. It was the sort of near-death experience from which many charities do not recover.

The funder takes control. Another charity found a very generous donor who promised the charity a small fortune, by its standards. As part of the deal, the charity installed the donor as chair. This led to the charity refocusing, which is not unreasonable. A few months later the

*The author was chair of this charity when DfID changed direction.

donor walked out and the expected payments stopped. If you depend on the whims of one person, you are in a very vulnerable position.

The charity becomes fat and lazy. Large is rarely lean. Bureaucracy takes over slowly like a boa constrictor squeezing its prey to death. But too much money can also harm a small charity. One startup received backing from a billionaire. It was chump change to the billionaire but a fortune to the charity. It proceeded to invest in a programme which generated great results. This was no surprise as the cost of the intervention per person was about the same as the annual income per person in the country they worked in. With less money they would have been more creative and more focused in designing a programme which could be scaled, instead of designing a gold-plated proof of concept which could not be scaled.

The charity loses direction. This is common where the government is the main partner and funder. Inevitably, government will want two things which are unhelpful to you. First, they will want more value for money, where value is always interpreted as lower cost, not better outcomes. This leads to death by a thousand cuts* until you eventually become hollowed out and ineffective. Second, they will want you to support the latest government policies: they will put in ever more stringent and obscure requirements about what you must deliver and where. It is very hard to say no to your major funder, especially if you are subject to competitive tender.

Ensure that you do not become too dependent on any one source of funding. If more than 20 per cent of your funding comes from one source, you are becoming dependent.

6. Unsustainability

Sustainability means matching the scale and scope of your operations to your funding capacity. Clearly, these factors are related: if you want to scale your operations you either have to scale your funding

---

*This is the pressure Teach First has suffered and is attempting to resist. The author is co-founder of Teach First.

or you must reduce and focus your scope of operations. Reducing scope does not mean achieving less. It means finding more creative ways of achieving the same amount with less resource – for instance through partnerships, stripping out unnecessary activity or smart cost reductions.

The simplest way to think about this is with an equation:

(Cost of delivery per beneficiary) x (number of beneficiaries) = cost of programme

In this equation, a beneficiary may be an individual, or it might be a whole school or community. And the cost should not just be the direct cost of the programme: you have to allow for all the support overheads which enables the programme to be delivered. Once you have calculated this, you can quickly see if you have a scalable and sustainable programme.

It is standard practice for charities to start out with a high-cost intervention and then reduce it dramatically as it scales. STIR started with a cost per child of $10, which was unscalable if you want to reach 300 million children every year. The cost is now under 30 cents per child and still falling.

To escape the sustainability trap you can either re-engineer your operations to deliver the same impact at much lower cost or raise your sustainable income levels. This requires a close understanding of your potential funder's willingness and ability to fund, or you have to find alternative sources of funding: earned income, legacies, government grants, retail fund raising.

7. Underinvestment

This is the sin which encompasses all the other sins. If you invest properly in finance and other support functions, you are unlikely to fall victim to any of the sins of money. But, as ever, entrepreneurs and funders prefer to invest in programmes, which means that they leave the organizational capacity of the charity very weak.

Money and finance are the engine of success. Invest in the people and systems to make sure you can manage them properly.

BUILD A SUSTAINABLE INCOME STREAM

Sustainable income is the Holy Grail which all not-for-profits seek. It is far harder than for-profit firms, which will normally have relatively stable sources of income. In practice, you have five main sources of potential income. You will probably rely on a mixture of the five sources to survive, although you will need to focus your efforts mainly on one (or possibly two) income streams. You cannot be effective in all five sources of income generation. Financially, diverse income streams are attractive. Operationally, focused income generation is more effective.

Each income stream has its advantages and drawbacks and will include:

1. Market place activity, as a social enterprise
2. Government funding
3. Grant funding from large donors
4. Retail donations
5. Payments By Results (PBR), Social Impact Bonds (SIB) and other new forms of hybrid performance-based funding
6. Portfolio of funding streams.

1. Market place activity, as a social enterprise

True social enterprises operate just like private sector firms, but reinvest all their surplus or profit into the social mission instead of paying dividends to shareholders. This has all the attractions and disciplines of running a for-profit business, with its focus on winning and keeping customers and serving them economically. It is a sustainable business model because you do not rely on the whims of governments and funders who may pull you in the wrong direction and then drop you, but there is usually a trade-off: the more you focus on commercial success, the harder it is to keep focus on your charitable goals.

THE EDEN PROJECT

The Eden Trust runs the Eden Project in Cornwall. One of the biggest tourist attractions in the area, it has attracted over 20 million paying visitors since 2000 and employs nearly 500 people in the area. Yet it is a social enterprise, its purpose is not to make a profit. It sets out to educate the public about humans' impact on, and dependence on, the flora (and fauna) of the world. It promotes a more sustainable way of living and is also an enjoyable day out.

Running the attraction and its educational schemes is expensive: over £30 million a year.* That's beyond the scope of any fundraising effort. Like any charity, The Eden Trust relies on a mixture of income sources. The main source of income is from paid admissions to the site, plus their spending on catering and gifts. It raises another 10 per cent of income from big grants, which help fund investment in new exhibits. And finally, it manages to avoid significant costs by using the services of nearly 200 volunteers over the season. Cost avoidance is as valuable as revenue generation.

Running the Eden Project like a business is the only realistic way to make it sustainable economically. It has been a huge success. The trade-off is between commercial versus charitable activities: how far should it focus on enjoyment versus education? In theory, it achieves both at the same time, but in practice, it is a difficult tightrope to walk.

---

*Eden Project Ltd Annual Report, 2022–23. Visitor numbers declined from 1 million pre-pandemic to just over 700,000 in 2023. Having a strong commercial operation brings its own challenges.

Creating a social enterprise still requires that you get the business model right: market discipline does not assure success. For instance, VisionSpring, focusing on central America, wanted to reach 300,000 people a year with eyeglasses by 2018. They realized that good eyesight would open the way to economic self-sufficiency for some of the poorest in society who could not afford eye tests and glasses. To achieve this scale of operation, they targeted 100 per cent cost recovery: a true social enterprise. To do this, they would require up to 300 stores, complete with a standardized and low-cost customer experience. This was a massive scaling operation: until 2014, VisionSpring had operated through a handful of stores which were locally run, agile and lean: they did what worked locally and there was no overhead.

VisionSpring soon ran into trouble. The standardized scale-up model sounded great in theory, but in practice it added far too much overhead, which they could not recover. Operating 300 stores on a centralized basis is very different to operating through a handful of stores at arm's length. They discovered that they did not have the relevant retail skills and feared that their stores might simply be competing with existing low-cost private sector operators. Early into expansion, they realized they were on the wrong track and made the courageous decision to close down and hand their expansion grants back to their funders. If you are going to engage with the market, you need to have the right business model and the right skills.

VisionSpring reverted to a more traditional NGO model. In 2022,[*] it had $12 million income which was split roughly 80/20 between donations and earned income: beneficiaries pay about one day of wages for glasses which can raise their income by 30 per cent. If you are a tea picker or clothes worker, for example, good eyesight has big impact on your earnings.

Grameen Bank and BRAC are unusual in that they can operate 100 per cent commercially. In practice, you may find it hard to

---

[*]VisionSpring Annual Report, 2023. The numbers are distorted by recovery from the pandemic, and exclude a $15 million donation from MacKenzie Scott.

achieve 100 per cent cost recovery. A more typical example is the One Acre Fund, which argues that it operates at the very bottom of the pyramid. They serve the poorest of the poor in remote areas which even Grameen struggles to reach. One Acre Fund does not target the extreme poor (under $1.90 income a day), they target the ultra-poor (under $0.5 income per day).* Their goal, like Grameen, is to help these farmers raise their incomes through financial and non-financial support. At first, they targeted 100 per cent cost recovery, but in 2017 found it was unrealistic for three reasons:

- The target population has very low knowledge levels and needs intensive support, which is costly;
- External factors such as drought, plant disease and conflict increase the level of support needed;
- Growth is costly, because new districts need more intense support than established ones.

Instead of focusing on cost recovery, One Acre Fund now focuses on SROI: social return on investment. They calculate the average improvement in a farmer's income compared to the average cost of intervention. Ideally, each dollar invested should raise farmers' incomes by $3 to $5.† This is still a commercial way of thinking, but removes the explicit requirement to make a surplus. Their deficit has to be covered by fund raising.

Nearly all social enterprises still depend on some element of fund raising to support growth, innovation and investment. Working as a social enterprise not only reduces your dependence on funders' whims, but also makes scaling possible.

---

*This definition of extreme versus ultra-poor is used by BRAC and by the United Nations, although the definition is contestable. For instance: https://www.un.org/development/desa/dspd/wp-content/uploads/sites/22/2017/04/Lamia-Rashid-BRAC-Ultrapoor-Graduation-Paper-for-UN-Expert-Group-Meeting-May-2017-25Apr17.pdf
†One Acre Fund Annual Report, 2023: https://oneacrefund.org/about-us/reports/annual-report

BRIDGE INTERNATIONAL ACADEMIES

Bridge is a private sector firm and demonstrates that you do not have to be a charity to have social impact. It started by offering low-cost private schooling in Kenya, Uganda, Nigeria and India. In 2016, Bridge signed a Public Private Partnership (PPP) deal with the government of Liberia to pilot a 50-school experiment of delivering the Bridge model in a public schools' setting. After seven years it is now working across all 15 counties in Liberia.[*]

Bridge has a unique vision of how to deliver education at low cost ($6.60 per child per month for tuition, plus add-ons for uniforms, meals, transport, exams and school materials). All teaching materials are prepared centrally and distributed by tablet, which then track the progress each teacher makes with each lesson. This remote monitoring and evaluation is supported by roving teams which provide additional teacher training and support where required.

Bridge's insight is that education can be a scalable business if you standardize and centralize the main inputs. Standardized lessons allow Bridge to hire unqualified teachers, often in areas where no teachers may be available. It also allows them to pay less than qualified teachers. Inevitably, the model is subject to criticism. In not allowing teachers to deviate from script, it becomes hard to identify great teachers from average. In randomized control trials, this approach shows students achieve an extra 2.5 years of learning within three years. The Bridge Model remains highly controversial, especially because of its for-profit focus.[†]

Although Bridge can make a profit on continuing operations, they need capital to fund development work. For this, they raised

---

[*] https://bridgeliberia.org/read-more-about-bridge-liberia/
[†] https://frontpageafricaonline.com/news/liberia-bridge-liberia-promised-to-solve-liberias-education-crisis-six-years-on-schools-are-still-failing/#google_vignette This is a fairly representative critique of Bridge.

$85 million on the equity market and $10 million in debt. This accelerates the path to scale in a way which traditional charities cannot match because they do not have access to capital markets. Bridge has also been able to get funding grants from the UK's aid agency, DfID.[*]

2. Government funding

The good news about governments is that they have a lot of money, the bad news is that you have to dance to their tune. There are two ways of interacting with government: reactive and proactive.

Reactive government relationships. This is where you reactively respond to whatever agenda the government may have. This makes you a government contractor: you attempt to win competitive tenders. You are likely to be competing with other for-profit and not-for-profit organizations.

A good example of this sort of relationship is Education Development Trust (EDT). The bulk of its £91 million income[†] comes from providing educational services to governments in the UK and around the world. All of these services are subject to tender periodically. Although it is a charity, it has to operate commercially to stay in business. By having a few areas of excellence in its services, such as school inspections, English language teaching and careers guidance, it is able to remain competitive. But the challenge comes in having a distinctive mission of its own which reaches beyond the mission of staying in business. Because it always has to respond to the agendas and tenders of governments, it is hard for it to create a distinctive agenda of its own. Working with government allows EDT to achieve scale, but makes it harder for EDT to pursue its own distinctive agenda.

[*]DfID was the Department for International Development at the time. It has now been reorganized and renamed FCDO: the Foreign, Commonwealth and Development Office.
[†]EDT Annual Report, 2023, p. 33. The author was also international chair of EDT before the pandemic.

Proactive government relationships. Most charities have a clear mission and sense of what they want to achieve. In their ideal world, they would proactively convince government to adopt their programme and take it to scale. This is where the charity provides the vital role of being the R&D lab for government and government becomes the scaling partner. This partnership model has been covered earlier in Chapter 4 on partnerships. This route to scale is powerful but dangerous. There are some basic ground rules you have to follow:

- Understand the government's agenda. Adapt your offering so that it clearly supports what government is trying to achieve. Focus on their needs, not your wants.
- Build a strong network of champions and supporters across government. If you rely on one person, you are at risk when restructurings or elections come along.
- Work the budget cycle. There are times when you have to stake your claim and other times when it is pointless. You also need to know where the pots of money are: your network should guide you to the right time, place and person.
- Let your government partners take all the credit and media coverage in good times, protect them in tough times.
- Be clear about where you add value and focus on that.
- Build real competence in managing government relations: it could be your magic sauce.

Your proactive relationship with government can follow one of two main strategies: direct scaling or adoption.

Direct scaling is where government funds your programme directly and you expand it. This seems very attractive, especially for ambitious founders and boards for whom scale is a measure of success. In practice, this puts you at the mercy of government's changing and shifting agenda. The government is unlikely to fund you without strings attached. Over time, you are likely to find the strings become increasingly tight and knotty, and it is hard to escape. You become a surrogate government department.

Adoption is where you build the intervention with government from the start, with a view to letting government take over and deliver the programme at scale. This has three main benefits:

- The programme will be tailored to the needs of the government
- Government will own the programme and be committed to it
- Funding looks after itself because government is funding its own programme.

As with every funding model, adoption by government is not a free lunch because it has significant drawbacks:

- Quality control: government is unlikely to have the passion and zeal of the NGO.
- Loss of control: government may change direction at any time.
- Role of the NGO: is there a role for the NGO after government adoption? Potentially there is, around continuing to innovate; training and support; monitoring and evaluation and running a demonstration district to show what excellent delivery looks like.

VILLAGEREACH

The VillageReach organization addresses the challenge of last-mile health care in remote and poor districts of Mozambique. It has a proactive government relationship: it has a clear mission and works with government to deliver it.

VillageReach started with a direct scaling approach. They worked out how to build a last-mile supply chain for vaccinations.

This is highly complex: it requires a secure cold chain with well-maintained equipment at every stage, reliable transport on poor roads, good use of tracking data to minimize wastage and assess outcomes; also, well-trained staff across the supply chain who can make good real-time decisions based on local circumstances.

Initial pilots provided a good proof of concept: it showed improved health outcomes, but also showed how complex and costly scaling would become. This was not something an NGO could sustainably deliver at national level – Mozambique is far larger than France – so it pivoted strategy to working with government to adopt the programme. This changes the role of VillageReach from being a delivery agent to building capacity and designing solutions for the government. As with many adoption models, establishing the proof of concept was a vital first step to demonstrate the viability of the programme.

Working at national scale sustainably can be logistically and financially impossible for an NGO: when the government adopts the programme, financial and logistical problems disappear and the role of the NGO has to change radically.*

3. Grant funding from large donors (B2B funding)

Foundations and philanthropists provide a vital funding service. They will fund things which are not fundable by other routes. Different foundations may provide one or more of the following sorts of funding (although none provide all these sorts of funding):

- Initial startup funding
- Funding for new ideas and innovations within an established charity
- Capital funding for infrastructure and buildings

*VillageReach Annual Report, 2023. https://www.villagereach.org/our-impact/governance-and-financials/ Currently, VillageReach reaches 73 million people with vaccinations and primary healthcare.

- Patient capital, where money spent now may not yield results for some years
- Scale-up funding to help you deliver a proof of concept.

They are also attractive funding partners because they will make decisions relatively quickly and transparently: they will tell you what they will and will not fund. Finally, the cost of fund raising is low financially. The financial cost of putting together a pitch is close to zero; the real cost is in the time and effort it takes to get to know the foundation and to produce an appropriate funding request.

It is rare for a cold pitch to work: simply sending in a request for funding is likely to be ignored. You have to invest time in getting to know the foundation and to understand what they really look for. The basics can be gleaned from their website: if you offer health services in Africa, there is no point in asking for money from a foundation that focuses on poverty relief in Asia. It is only when you start talking to the grant officers or the trustees that you can properly understand their motivations. As you talk with them, you can effectively co-design your grant application. When they finally receive it, they will be expecting it and you will have answered all their questions and objections in the document. You have to invest time with your donors to build an effective relationship.

The risks of donor funding are similar to government funding:

Mission creep. It is easy to land up chasing the money instead of chasing the mission. Every grant is a compromise between what you want to achieve and what your donor wants to achieve: alignment of goals, target groups and type of intervention are rarely complete. The more heavily you depend on one donor, the more you are at risk.

Unsustainability. Donors' priorities change and grant officers come and go with different agendas and ways of working. You are unlikely to receive a grant of more than three years, so you have to maintain strong relationships and track record if you want the grant to renew.

Impact. Funders, reasonably, like to see results from their funding. This will often force you to focus on delivering short-term results which address symptoms, not causes. If you want to deliver systemic change you need to find funders with the patience of a saint, great vision and great belief in what you are doing. These are not easy to find.

4. Retail donations (B2C funding)

Retail donations are attractive because they come with no strings attached, unless you specify that they are part of a specific appeal, such as aid for a natural disaster or funding to restore a historic building. These unrestricted funds are valuable: they give you maximum discretion on how to allocate your resources.

The challenges with retail donations are that they are expensive to attract and some charities have indulged in unsavoury practices to attract donations. Where grant funding from major donors appeals to the head, charities appeal to the hearts of retail donors. The classic appeal involves a doe-eyed child looking pitifully at you from a poster or letter with a message saying 'text £3 to save this child/save her eyesight/provide an education/give her shelter/get her vaccinated'. It takes a heart of stone not to feel moved by the plight of the child, but the fundraising is deceptive, at best. The £3 is not enough to save the world or save the child, and may not be used for that purpose at all: it may simply help buy a Frappuccino for a staff member, which is not quite such a compelling cause. And much of your £3 will have gone in fundraising costs. Guide Dogs for the Blind, which is eminently worthy, spends 33 per cent of its £100 million income on fundraising.[*]

The extreme end of retail funding can be ugly. Olive Cooke was a 92-year-old poppy seller[†] in the UK, who became overwhelmed by

[*]https://www.charityfinancials.com/charity-financials-insider/fundraising-how-much-does-it-really-cost-charities-1755.html
[†]In the UK poppy sellers sell artificial poppies to raise funds for ex-servicemen and are particularly active in the run-up to Remembrance Day on 11 November each year.

endless requests for donations.* Each request may have been reason-able, but collectively, they were very unreasonable. She received up to 3,000 mailed donation requests in a year because charities were selling and sharing details of donors. This tidal wave of requests contributed to depression and she eventually took her own life.

Retail donors have limited time or interest in understanding whether you have done a randomized control trial which demon-strates your impact. They will respond to an emotional cause which is close to their heart. As with any advertising pitch, you have to identify your target market, build a clear and simple message and then work out which are the most cost-effective channels to reach your target. This is classic marketing which requires strong marketing skills and significant budget: you need to do it well or not at all.

If you enter the retail funding market you need to balance the need to be effective with the need to be ethical.

5. *PBR, SIB and other new forms of hybrid performance-based funding*
More innovative forms of funding have emerged over the last few years, including Payment by Results (PBR) and Social Impact Bonds (SIB). In practice, the ideas are often linked. A Social Impact Bond is a bond which does not pay interest, but pays out depending on the outcomes achieved. In practice, the required outcomes and payouts are calibrated to give the investor a realistic probability of an attrac-tive return on their investment.

At best, innovative financing will enable innovative solutions to long-term problems. This was the goal of the world's first PBR initia-tive at Peterborough Prison (see box below). If the financing and incentives are correct, it will encourage multiple agencies to collabo-rate on solving a complex problem and will address the causes of the problem, not the symptoms.

*https://www.bbc.co.uk/news/uk-england-bristol-33550581

REDUCING RE-OFFENDING THROUGH PBR AND SIB*

The world's first social impact bond was launched in 2010 to fund a pilot programme aimed at reducing re-offending among short-term offenders in Peterborough, England. Short-term prisoners (sentences under 12 months) typically have the highest re-offending rates because the prisons have had little time to offer rehabilitation services to them.

Various foundations invested £5 million: they would get their capital and a bonus back if they could show that they had reduced re-offending by 7.5 per cent. This gave rise to serious measurement challenges, but eventually the UK government agreed that the first two cohorts had seen a reduction in re-offending by 9 per cent and full payment was made. Although the government released the results in 2017, they have chosen not to repeat or expand the experiment: they are less convinced about the results than the published data suggests.

The funding was used to integrate key rehabilitation services on a customized basis for each ex-offender: each person had different needs which required different interventions from Ormiston Families, Sova, MIND, TTG Training, YMCA and John Laing Training, among others. These providers were managed by St Giles Trust under the guidance of Social Finance.

PBR and SIB are not magic bullets: their effectiveness depends on how each contract is constructed. In several cases it has become clear that PBR contracts have been gamed. In another prison's PBR, the private contractors gamed the system perfectly:

- The contract had a base payment for running the prison plus a performance bonus for reducing re-offending. The

*This scheme was widely reported. The UK government evaluation was published on 27 July 2017: https://www.gov.uk/government/publications/final-results-for-cohort-2-of-the-social-impact-bond-payment-by-results-pilot-at-hmp-peterborough

base payment was less than the existing cost of running the prison, so government hoped this would focus the contractor on reducing re-offending.

- The contractor worked out that they could make a profit simply by reducing the cost of running the prison: if there was any reduction in re-offending that would be pure profit.
- To demonstrate their re-offending credentials, the contractors promised (small) work to charities working in the sector. The charities were simply bid candy to meet a condition in the tender document.
- No significant re-offending efforts were made, the contractors did not get their bonus, but they did make a profit.

The effectiveness of PBR and SIB is in the design of the contracts. It is still an emerging practice globally. Worldwide, there are fewer than 300 such projects in about 35 countries in 2024.* Mistakes will be made and money will be lost, but as funders, charities and governments discover what works, the market has the potential to grow.

For charities, this sector raises risks and opportunities. Ineffective charities will be left out in the cold and few will miss them. Effective charities will face a decision about where they play in this new market. A few charities, and many private firms, will want to step up into the role of prime contractor. The prime contractor holds the contract with government, takes the risk (and the profit), designs the programme, decides who else will deliver the programme and integrates their efforts. The prime contractor also holds all the cards, financially and operationally. Success requires a set of contract management and project management skills which few smaller charities have.

Your alternative is to remain as a tier two contractor. This works if you have a very specialist intervention which no one else can provide credibly. In this case, you will be able to persuade the main contractor

*The Government Outcomes Lab at the Blavatnik School of Government, Oxford University. https://golab.bsg.ox.ac.uk/knowledge-bank/indigo/impact-bond-dataset-v2/

to fund you properly with sensible terms and conditions. If you do not have a distinctive capability, life as a tier two contractor can be very uncomfortable. You will be squeezed on price and you will suffer difficult terms and conditions: the main contractor will happily transfer all the risk to you, impose onerous reporting requirements and performance metrics and delay payments.

6. Portfolio of funding streams

Most charities eventually develop a mixed portfolio of funding streams, which can be sustainable at very large scale. This is good risk management. Any single form of funding stream has its risks and drawbacks; collectively, you should be able to create a portfolio of funding streams which meet your needs. Each portfolio will be as unique as your mission.

PORTFOLIO FUNDING

Oxfam* had £400 million income in 2022/23. It sustains this level of funding through multiple funding channels, including:

- Institutional donors (governments, UN aid agencies, foundations): £156 million
- Donations and legacies (individual donations, legacies, appeals): £143 million
- Trading income from 650 shops and online, with £14 million profit from £98 million turnover.
- Investment income, £3 million.

As with many charities, it also has hidden income in the value of the services delivered by the thousands of volunteers who staff their shops and help out in other ways.

---

*Oxfam Annual Report, 2023.

Oxfam is something of an outlier in having such a well-balanced and diversified income stream. In practice, most charities have the capacity to build real expertise in one, or maybe two, streams of income generation: you cannot be good at everything. Research* on the top 297 US non-profits with over $50 million income showed that 90 per cent of them rely on one dominant category for the bulk of their revenue. If the largest non-profits find it necessary to focus their fundraising work, then focus is even more important for smaller non-profits. Smaller non-profits simply do not have the capacity or capability to achieve excellence in multiple income streams.

Your funding strategy will need to evolve over time. At startup, you will hustle for money and hustle to avoid costs. It is messy but effective. As you start to scale you need to formalize and professionalize your funding strategy. Eventually, you need a clear view of what long-term sustainability at scale looks like. This may lead to you radically changing how you operate: you may have to cut back and focus your operations, limit the spread of where you work, work with partners who can share the load with you and work to get government to adopt your idea.

Your funding strategy should not be an afterthought to your mission: it should be central to how you achieve and scale your mission.

MONEY: SUMMARY

The good news about money is that you need very little money to start up: the biggest ideas started with the smallest amounts of pocket money. The bad news is that everything else about money is far harder in an NGO than in the private sector:

---

*Kelley, A., Isom, D., Seeman, B., Silverman, J., Cuevas-Ferreras, A. & Frei-Herrmann, K. (2024). A New Look at How US Nonprofits Get Really Big, Stanford Social Innovation Review: https://doi.org/10.48558/HZ0S-ED29

- Growth is not a route to profit: it means you have to spin the fundraising wheel ever faster.
- You cannot borrow to invest or grow and you cannot raise equity.
- You have a lean operation with no safety net: costly mistakes (fraud, litigation, employment disputes) can be terminal.

Further bad news is that financial management plays to all the weaknesses of most NGO founders:

- Attention to detail, not the big picture
- Focus on controls and compliance, not on being entrepreneurial
- Selling to strangers, instead of delivering the programme on the ground.

You cannot change the world without money: you have to deal with it. This means you will need:

- A clear and sustainable financial strategy: know where your money will come from.
- Effective financial controls and management: hire a good financial team.
- A strong fund-raising funnel which you will have to lead in the early days, because partners always want to talk to the CEO.

6

Machine

Scale, sustain and replicate your impact

The heart of this chapter is showing how you can build a machine to scale, replicate and sustain the impact you want to achieve. Many entrepreneurs are free spirits and do not enjoy the disciplines of working with and for a machine. But if you want to change the world, you need a machine as surely as you need a machine to travel the world.

This chapter will show you how you can build a machine which works. Here, we will cover:

- *The five tests of a good machine: what it must achieve*
- *The seven elements of a good machine, and how you can build each one.*

Finally, we will explore how you can protect yourself and your organization against the bad stuff. Everyone likes to think that bad stuff happens to other people; entrepreneurs are optimists and are particularly likely to think this way. Bad stuff will happen to you: know how to prevent it and treat it. Do not let a crisis become a drama.

THE FIVE TESTS OF A GOOD MACHINE

You know you are on the path to success if you can scale, replicate and sustain your impact without being blown up by the bad stuff. These are the five goals your machine must deliver:

- Impact
- Scale
- Replication
- Sustainability
- Risk management.

Your constant mantra should be: 'How can I scale, replicate and sustain this impact?'

Impact: if you want to change the world, you need to make an impact. This might sound obvious, but in practice many NGOs lose focus. Survival of the organization takes precedence over the mission; the NGO starts to chase the money, which means meeting the needs of governments and funders who will pull you away from the heart of what you want to achieve. Loss of focus does not happen in one big event. It's a slow walk into irrelevance: each step of the way is entirely logical and then you find you are lost in a swamp.

Scale: your machine has to be able to take you to scale. That means it must be built so that normal professionals can reproduce your success without working 24/7 and without having your charisma, commitment and passion. Learn how to exploit the advantages of scale. Scale gives you the ability to hire more specialist skills; ability to learn from delivery with different products, services and geographies; ability to test more new ideas; ability to talk to bigger funders and catch the attention of policy makers. Meanwhile, you need to mitigate the problems of scale: excess overhead, bureaucracy, slow decision making and the emergence of people who appear to do nothing very useful.

Replication: you have to be able to replicate your machine and your success across different contexts and geographies. This means you need to understand what your magic sauce really is: this is what cannot be altered across geographies. Then understand how much you can flex everything else. The process of replication forces you to think about what is your core and what can be customized. It's a process of focusing your operations more and more. It raises inevitable questions about what can be done at the centre and what can be managed locally, which leads to equally inevitable friction between head office and front line.

Sustainability: this is mainly about finding a sustainable economic model. Sustaining your model when you are working with a few people is a relatively easy fund-raising task. Sustaining a global operation which is changing the world requires a completely different way of thinking, outlined in Chapter 5 on money.

Risk management is an entirely theoretical and pointless exercise until the bad stuff happens when it suddenly becomes very practical and purposeful. It is too late to start thinking about risk management when the risk has crystallized into a problem. Prevention is always better than cure, not least because some risks are fatal.

THE SEVEN ELEMENTS OF A GOOD MACHINE, AND HOW TO BUILD THEM

If you want to build a machine, it helps to have a blueprint to base it on. Below is a highly simplified blueprint for building your machine to change the world. It is useful because it gives you a framework to make sure that you are asking yourself the right questions about your organization. Every challenge you face will fall into one of the boxes below. The only exception is risk management: this could be treated as a process, but is sufficiently important to be given its own guide book.

Build your machine

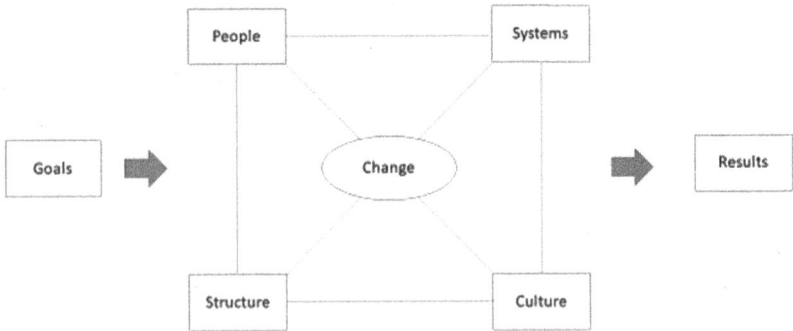

A blueprint with seven boxes and a few lines connecting them is not quite enough to build your machine. It helps if you also have an assembly manual to go with the blueprint. Below is a brief guide to each of the seven elements. Knowing the right questions is as important as knowing the right answer: a great answer to the wrong question is no use at all.

Goals

Goal setting is Management 101. How hard can it be, really?

As it turns out, goal setting is very hard indeed. Research on global teams* showed that goal setting was consistently rated as one of the five biggest problems every team faced, even among some of the largest and most professional firms in the world. The problems with goal setting are about both substance and process.

Substance

Setting goals is not black and white. You will always be working in the grey space of uncertainty. Even for-profit firms struggle with goal clarity: should we focus limited resources on marketing, R&D, customer service or production quality? These are marginal decisions. In the absence of the profit motive, it is much harder to set goals which allow you to make the critical, marginal decisions about where

---

*Original research published in *Global Teams* by Jo Owen, *Financial Times*, 2017.

to allocate resources and which actions you should take. This grey space is muddied by funders and stakeholders who keep on wanting to push and pull you in slightly different directions.

The more complexity and uncertainty exist, the more your team will value clarity and certainty. Complexity and uncertainty always increases as you descend through the organization. Slight ambiguity in messaging will lead to chaos and confusion at the front line. Your job is to make the complex simple and the uncertain certain. Many of the best CEOs reduce their goal focus to just one goal, which is often simply stated, as in the example below:

'FOCUS ON THE CLASSROOM'

Teach First had grown hugely successful. Part of its success included setting up an incubator which helped Teach First alumni develop new social enterprises that could change the world. Teach First set up the Fair Education Alliance, which brought together over 250 leading NGOs, corporates and think-tanks to share experience and develop a common vision of how to address education disadvantage.* They also built a leadership programme to help participants become leaders of the future and had an active ambassador movement of more than 10,000 alumni. Russell Hobby was appointed as a new CEO and saw that all these extra activities were good, but they added cost, complexity and confusion. His agenda was to refocus on the core mission of Teach First 'focus on the classroom'. That was his message and mission as the new CEO. This relentless focus had dramatic results. All the non-core activities were spun out; headcount and cost were reduced dramatically and recruitment numbers for the core mission increased. Everyone in the organization understood the priority and acted accordingly.

A simple message is the best message, and the best goal.

---

*Correct in 2024: https://www.faireducation.org.uk/

The best goal is not a repeat of your mission statement which might be 'save the Amazon forest' or 'eliminate childhood diseases' or 'reduce agricultural poverty'. Your mission statement may be clear, but how you get there is shrouded in fog. Your goal is likely to be a one- or two-year campaign which shows clearly what your next steps need to be on the journey towards your mission. More relevant goals for a year or two might be:

- *Professionalize the organization*: standardize delivery, stabilize operations, set up clear rhythms and routines for reporting, communicating, evaluating, decision making.
- *Focus on impact:* strip away unnecessary activity; identify more clearly users' needs; enhance monitoring and evaluation; encourage more innovation and testing.
- *Prepare for scale:* re-work the economic model to strip away what is not needed; find scaling partners; identify where to scale and who to work with for funding and delivery.

These simplistic goals give clarity and are a call to arms. They also show how you are going to make a difference as a leader: if you are not making a difference, you are not leading. These goals do not mean that you stop doing everything else, they simply give a sense of priority. Once the goal has been fixed at the top level, it can be cascaded through the organization into ever more detail at each level.

Process

If the substance of goal setting is hard, the process is harder.

CEOs can often be found whining that their organization does not understand what they are meant to do and they are not show-ing commitment to the right direction. If the CEO wants to find the source of the problem, look in the mirror. There is good reason why teams struggle to internalize your thoughts. You may have spent months working on a strategy and set of goals. By the end of count-less discussions with your top team and your board, you will have understood all the trade-offs, risks and rationale for your decision.

You then announce the goal to great fanfare at an event and to rein-force the message you might hold some workshops to flesh it out. There is no way that mere mortals can internalize months of debate in a 20-minute speech and one-hour workshop. Your team are not mind readers. You have to help them understand your thoughts.

If you communicate your goal after setting it, you are communi-cating it too late.

The process of buy in to a new direction has to start well before the direction is set. You need to involve the wider organization in the discussion from an early stage, even if you think you have the answer pre-wrapped and packaged in your head already. The discussion may be closed, not open. Asking 'what should our goal for the next two years be?' is open, democratic and weak. Instead, you might ask 'how might we go about preparing for scale?' This is closed, directed and more useful. You will immediately start to get feedback about chal-lenges, opportunities, sources of confusion and main priorities as different groups see them. You can start to shape your goal appro-priately: the overall goal may not change much, but the detail and messaging will become more tailored to the needs of each part of the organization. The discussion process also ensures that you have buy in even before you get on stage and announce the plan at your big event. People rarely argue with an idea when they think it is their own.

This buy-in process is not just internal. Invite funders and other key stakeholders into your strategy conversations. They are vital for two reasons. First, they will normally have a huge wealth of experi-ence to draw on. They will be able to tell what works, what does not work and where the big trade-offs are. Second, their buy in is essen-tial to your future. If they have been part of the process, they are far more likely to understand and support what you are doing. Funders are more likely to fund you when they feel involved and truly under-stand what you are doing.

This 'fair process' goal setting and decision making takes time and effort. It is an investment worth making. It means you move from deci-sion to action very fast. The Japanese have a word for it: *nemawashi*, which is the process of building consensus behind the scenes. When everyone comes to the decision-making meeting, they are not making a decision: they are confirming in public the agreements they have made in private. From there to action is fast. Being slow to decide and fast to act is better than the opposite: fast to decide and slow to act, where everyone tries to undo or re-prosecute the decision after you have made it. That is a recipe for conflict and inaction.

Goal setting may be Management 101, but it really can be hard.

Systems

Entrepreneurs are often disrupters. They are free spirits who rarely have much time for bureaucracy. In the early days, the visionary leader is vital to leading the revolution. Before and after the revolution you do not need radical visionaries changing the world: you need the reliable komissars who make sure that the trains run on time and that the bread gets delivered. To do that, you need systems which are reliable and predictable. In other words, you need bureaucracy.

Most social entrepreneurs struggle with this transition. In the early days, they do not need formal systems. If there are just five of you working in a shared office then everyone knows what everyone else is doing. When you grow, you need to professionalize the organization. You need reliable systems for managing people, projects, money and decisions. A few of the questions you will need to answer include:

- People: how can we hire the right people, how can we evaluate them, what should their terms and conditions be, what career path should they have, how do we deal with performance and disciplinary issues, how can we train, develop, retain and motivate our staff, how can we develop an employee handbook?
- Projects: how can we track progress effectively and how can we learn what works and what does not work; do we have the right M&E in place to meet the needs of funders and stakeholders?
- Money: what is the scheme of delegation: who has authority to approve what and for how much? Have we got effective

separation of duties, do we have proper controls to prevent fraud and waste, are the controls actually enforced, what are our policies on expenses and how do we track and report on budget by project? Are we clear on cash flow, accruals, forecasting and budget setting and tracking? Do we have a risk log which helps us manage financial and non-financial risks well?

- Decisions: who has decision-making rights over what decisions; who is accountable and responsible for what, what does fair process in decision making look like and how should people be kept informed?

Usually, these systems are developed in response to a problem. After making a few false hires, you soon learn the value of a clear hiring process and criteria, backed up by taking references. The one area where it is not worth waiting to react to problems is with financial systems. Financial problems can put you out of business very fast.

SO YOU THINK THE BAD STUFF ONLY HAPPENS TO OTHER PEOPLE…

Good financial systems alone will not achieve your mission, but poor financial systems can destroy your mission. I used to believe that the bad stuff only happened to other people. Fate can be a cruel teacher, as I found out at one charity:

- Our first financial manager was incompetent, with the result that we had no cash to make payroll in ten days' time. We survived to learn the value of cash flow forecasting and fired the manager.
- The next manager was competent enough to manage cash flow, but not competent enough to get away with signing cheques to himself. Our bank controls picked that up. We fired that manager and discovered the value of segregation of duties.
- The next manager was competent and popular, not least because she had a side hustle of selling cheap luxury goods to colleagues.

She held a party at her flat, where we found she kept large amounts of cash in shoe boxes: she said she did not trust banks, which was odd for a financial manager. We found out why she did not trust banks on the day she did not turn up for work: she had been arrested for helping an armed gang rob a bank. We learned the value of taking up references on new hires.

At other charities I have had the joy of dealing with false supplier invoice fraud, determined external fraud attempts and not infrequent cheating on expenses and petty embezzlement. Ninety-nine per cent of people are trustworthy and honest, 1 per cent can destroy your charity: make sure you have your defences in place.

Building these systems is an organic process. If you try to create them from day zero, you will create a bureaucratic monster. You will spend your whole time serving the machine, not serving the mission. But if you build systems too slowly, you will have destructive chaos.

Three things will help you build the right systems at the right time:

- The right support. It helps if you have people on your board, or other advisors, who have helped other organizations achieve scale. They will know what good looks like and they will also understand your journey: they will not attempt to impose large corporate solutions on a small startup.
- The right mindset. If you think of systems as bureaucracy, you will fight systems. Instead, think of them as professionalizing the organization and building a machine which will take your mission to scale. The right machine will free up your time to focus where you need to focus. Instead of firefighting, you and your team will have predictable rhythms and routines for dealing with all the noise of day-to-day management.
- The right frameworks. You do not need to invent all these systems and processes from scratch. Many other charities have already done the hard work for you. Usually, you can

find friendly charities to share their employee handbooks, schemes of delegation and other processes with you: you can then adapt their systems for your needs.

Culture

At random, here is one corporate values statement: can you identify the firm from the values statement?

- Customer commitment
- Quality
- Integrity
- Teamwork
- Respect for people
- Good citizenship
- A will to win
- Personal accountability.

There are two main problems with this:

- It is far too long: no one can remember eight values, let alone act on them, measure them and enforce them.
- It is completely generic: they are values which could apply more or less anywhere. It gives no idea about what is distinctive about this firm.

The firm in question is a global financial services firm. They have recently switched from another set of eight generic values. The real test of their values, and any values anywhere, has nothing to do with what is written down on paper. Those are simply the guiding beliefs that worthy senior executives have spent a huge amount of time crafting. The real values and real culture of the organization are captured by how people behave when they think no one is watching. The right culture induces people to behave and act the right way when you are not there and are not looking.

An antidote to the financial services firm is Google. It started life with a very simple values statement: 'Don't be Evil.' In 2015, Alphabet updated this with 'Do the right thing.' This is simple enough that everyone can understand it, remember it and act on it. If it forces debate occasionally about 'what is the right thing to do now?', that is very useful.

Your challenge is to create a culture which is fit for purpose. This is a bit like bottling fog. Initially, the values of the organization will be your values, for better or for worse. Over time, you will find that the culture and the organization assume a life of their own. Norms start developing and then they start shifting as you grow. You need to find a way of training the beast called culture. You have three main tools at your disposal:

- Hire to values, not just to skills. You can train skills, you cannot train values.
- Promote and recognize values as much as performance. If you promote people who get outcomes by any means possible, then staff will do what it takes. Integrity and decency will fly out of the window.
- Act according to your values, especially at moments of truth. Colleagues watch you closely all the time. How you act is how they learn to act.

Hiring and promotion are covered further in the next section of this chapter, on people. The true test of your values is how you act when the chips are down. For instance, STIR has four values of which 'Openness' is one. At first, that value might elicit a big yawn but when the chips are down, it changes how teams and leadership act. The way openness is interpreted is 'radical candour in real time'. Here is how it changes behaviour:

- Serious external fraud: share the problem with funders immediately; work with them to find a solution.

- Misconduct in an office: be open about the problem, work with staff to reset the values.
- Strategy development: don't keep it secret. Open the process up to advice from funders, stakeholders and staff alike.

Staff do not believe what you say, they believe what you do. They watch the feet, not the mouth. As a leader, the team will take their cues from you. So if you wonder why the values of your NGO are not values you like, start by looking in the mirror.

People: your team

As with systems and culture, you will find the nature of the people you hire and work with changes over time. This change is often traumatic for you, the organization and those around you. Put simply, very few of your startup team will land up being your scaling team and even fewer will be around when you reach scale. Different sorts of people fit different stages of growth and you have to manage each transition.

In the early days you will need entrepreneurial people who can do anything and everything: they need to be able to hustle and make things happen with little or no money. They have to enjoy the freedom and uncertainty which comes with ambiguity and lack of clear rules and processes. They are not classic corporate types of people.

Early success leads to the downfall of your startup team. As you grow, you need to build a machine which is scalable, sustainable and replicable. You start to need policies and procedures. This will enrage your startup team. One by one they will come to you and tell you that your startup is losing the magic culture which enabled it to succeed; they will tell you it is doomed and then they will leave. These are sad, painful and inevitable discussions. Do not try to appease your startup team; do not pretend that everything will be the same. Change is necessary, and that means your team will have to change as well.

In practice, as you grow and professionalize you will find that you can hire more expert staff. Your roles will become more specialized, which makes it easier to target your recruitment. And as you grow, you become less of an unknown and risky employer: you will attract higher-calibre professionals who can help you with your next stage of development.

People: yourself
If startup people are rarely the right people for scaling, where does that leave you when your organization starts to grow?

Most founders are leaders, not managers. They have the vision and the energy to make things happen. The day-to-day hard graft of management is less appealing. Managing people, egos, careers, disputes, performance and the daily misunderstandings of organizational life is vital, but not energizing. If you do not like this sort of work, you will not be good at it. Fortunately, there is a solution: don't do this work. Find someone else who can manage the shop for you: hire a COO (chief operating officer). Leadership is a team sport, and your first priority should be to build a team to help you succeed.

As your organization grows, you should constantly be promoting yourself in role. Your title (CEO) may never change, but what you do will keep on changing in one direction. You will find that you focus more and more on less and less. Focus on what no one else can do for you. In practice, this probably means you focus on stakeholder management externally and on strategy internally. You become cheerleader-in-chief for your startup. Everything else, someone else can do for you.

The theory is simple, but the practice is difficult because founders find it very hard to let go. Essentially, they do not want to trust anyone else with their baby. The founder has plenty of personal evidence to show that no one else can be trusted: it was your idea, not someone else's; your success will have proven many doubters wrong. Why should you trust other people's judgement? This quickly becomes a vicious circle: the less you trust others with big decisions, the harder it becomes to recruit and retain a great team which merits your trust. If you cannot trust your team, then either you have the wrong team or the team has the wrong leader. Either way, the problem is yours to fix.

At some point, you not only need to step back, you need to step out. This is the hardest decision of all. Overstaying your welcome is risky because:

- You become identified with the organization and the organization becomes identified with you. That is unhealthy for both sides.
- The organization becomes too dependent on you, internally and externally.
- It is hard to challenge an over-mighty founder, who probably does not welcome challenge. That leads to poor decision making and makes it hard to retain top talent.
- Eventually, the founder grows bored of business as usual and wants new diversions: grandiose new projects, becoming famous on the speaking circuit or joining prestigious committees and commissions.

Moving on becomes very hard to do. Success is very comfortable and you will have painful memories of just how hard and risky it is to start all over again. You know that you are a tough act to follow: second acts require courage.

Overstaying is rarely good for you or for your organization. Be clear in your own mind what success looks like and then give yourself a time frame to achieve your goal. You should not need more than seven years to see your idea through to success. If it takes longer, it may need fresh thinking and fresh talent to move it forwards. If you deliver success within seven years, you can declare victory and move on to your next thing. It is better to move on your terms than wait for your board to make the decision for you.

Structure (board and governance)

Here is what you need to know about structure:

- There is no perfect structure. Build the structure around your team: it is better to have slightly sub-optimal structure than to have a slightly sub-optimal team.
- The right structure is context specific: that means the structure has to change as you grow and change.
- NGO structures are more porous than corporate structures. You rely far more on partnerships, volunteers and other stakeholders than most firms. Your structure, systems, processes and culture need to be flexible enough to adapt.
- The most challenging part of the structure is your governance. Governance is the focus of this section on structure.

Here, we will focus on governance, because that's what most often goes wrong. Once it goes wrong, it is very hard to correct since you have no formal power over the board. Informally, you have huge power.

Although the board has formal power to direct the executive and to hire and fire, in practice most boards are very reluctant to exercise their legal powers. Firing a CEO is a nightmare: finding a new CEO is very time-consuming and risky. Most boards do not have time and do not enjoy risk. This means that the executive has control. Which raises the obvious question: what is the point of the board?

WHEN GOVERNANCE GOES WRONG

We were starting up, which meant we focused on the normal deluge of challenges: raising funds, finding a team, blagging resources, building a website, persuading stakeholders to back us and finding a desk to work at. Fortunately, a kindly elder statesman came along and offered to deal with all the tedious administration of setting

---

up the corporate structure and dealing with the regulators, officials and lawyers. We readily agreed: we had more pressing matters to deal with.

Mistake. Big Mistake.

The kindly gentleman used this administrative work to insert himself as chairman and his friends as trustees. He had effected an administrative coup on us, which would not have mattered if he had been any good. But he was not. He spent the next six years trying to hold us back, because he was very risk-averse and wanted an easy life. Eventually, he disappeared; the charity could finally recover and grow.

In the absence of shareholders, the trustees (specifically the members of the charity) own the organization and can hire and fire the team. They can be a great force for good or ill. Make sure you put the right governance with the right people in place from the start.

At minimum, every board has a set of fiduciary duties to make sure that the charity is run well. This is tedious work for the board and it is tedious for the executive to prove that it is doing the right thing in terms of financial controls and management, regulatory compliance and risk management. If this is all the board does, it adds very little value and the executive will regard the board as just another obstacle which they have to overcome.

In practice, you can make the board an asset for the organization. Here's what a board can do for you:

- Provide funding. This is dangerous: when funders are on the board they can take control and push the NGO in a direction which suits them. It is hard to say no to a major funder who sits on the board.
- Provide access to power, money and partners. This can be very useful, but many prospective board members talk a

better game than they deliver. Make sure that they are both willing and able to make their network work for you.
- Provide skills. Board members cannot do the work for you, but they can help you do it better. The right board will have the experience and knowledge to know what works and what does not; they can become unpaid and high-value coaches to you and your leadership team.

The skills-based board is likely to be the most active board, which provides help to you and your team between board meetings. The danger is that executive and non-executive roles can become blurred. There has to be clarity that outside board meetings trustees can observe and learn. They can offer help and advice, but they can never give direction. Outside the board meetings, board members are servants and not masters of the executive.

The most important board choice is the choice of chair. If you are starting up, you can choose your chair. If there is a chair succession then the board chooses the new chair, but you should ensure that you influence the choice of chair. The vital requirement is that you should be so close to your chair in public, not even a slip of paper can squeeze between the two of you. You have to give each other 100 per cent support in public. This will allow you to have very robust discussions in private, safe in the knowledge that private disagreements will not become public. The chair should then be able to deliver the support of the rest of the board for whatever you agree in private.

Change

At the heart of your machine is change. Your machine constantly has to adapt to changing circumstances. Most people sign up to the idea that change is vital, but they prefer change to happen to other people. In reality, change involves extra work and extra personal risk, which is why so many people resist change in practice. Your challenge is to be able to keep the NGO progressing and changing as it needs to. The key is to make sure that change is not done *to* your team, but is done *with* your team.

You will know if you have set up change for success if you have managed the following five ingredients of success:

- Vision. Have a clear vision of what change will deliver, not just for the NGO but also for each team member. Change is personal. Team members want to know what's in it for them. There may well be winners and losers: winners stay quiet, losers shout loudly.
- Need. Show why there is a need for change. The need for your NGO to change may be obvious, but the need for an individual team member to change their role, objectives or reporting line may be less clear. It often helps to show that there is a burning platform. If the choice is between changing your reporting line or losing your job, most people will choose to change their reporting line.
- Credibility. If you always preach change and never do anything, then your team will stop listening. Show that you are serious and make sure that you have the capacity and capability to make change happen. Always do as you say.
- First steps. The easiest thing to do is nothing. Passive resistance kills change. You have to build momentum. Once people see the train is leaving the station, they can get on it or stay behind or even jump on the tracks in front of the train. Usually, people choose to join the train: it can be very lonely if you are left behind on the platform.
- Risks. All change involves risk. The easy risk is rational risk for the NGO, which can be captured and dealt with in risk logs. The real risk is personal: 'how will I be affected by this?' People will cloak personal risk in rational terms. Cut through the smokescreen. Understand how change affects each team member and manage their hopes and fears appropriately.

Be aware that as the founder and CEO, change may be exciting to you. It is also largely risk-free because you are in control of the change and you are unlikely to write yourself out of a role. But your team will not share your passion for upheaval, distraction, extra work and extra risk. The NGO may need to keep on changing and growing, but you have to manage change so that it is a journey which your team can also manage.

MACHINE: SUMMARY

An effective machine will allow you to scale, replicate and sustain impact while managing risk. Most entrepreneurs do not enjoy building or running machines. Find a COO and a team which can build and run the machine for you.

The five key elements of the machine for you to work on are:

- Goals. These need to be clear, not just to you, but to your team. That means you have to involve them in setting the goals so that they own them and understand not only what the goals are but also why they have been chosen.
- Systems which are about creating the rhythms and routines of decision making, reporting and information sharing. These routines avoid confusion and re-work, and simplify and focus the efforts of everyone.
- People. A great mission requires great people. Hire to values, not just to skills. As the NGO grows, bring in more specialized professionals. Some of the startup team will grow in role, be ready for many others leaving in protest at what they see as creeping bureaucracy.
- Culture is how people behave when you are not watching. Focus on the two or three behaviours which will make the most difference to achieve sustainable impact. A long values statement is worthy but irrelevant: if it cannot be remembered, it cannot be managed.
- Structure. There is no such thing as the perfect structure, there is only what works in context. The vital part of structure which

---

NGOs miss at their peril is effective governance. Make sure you have governance which adds the value you need: skills, money or access.

These five elements of your machine keep on changing, but most people do not really like change because it involves personal risk and extra work. Change is not just about the needs of the NGO. Focus on the needs of your team: show why change is necessary from their personal perspective, how it will help them and how they can be part of the change process. Change should be done *with* people, not *to* them.

7

From worm's- to bird's-eye view of the world

Charities, NGOs and aid agencies waste a huge amount of time, effort and money. This is well known at a policy level. The challenge of waste is even more acute when seen from the worm's-eye view: waste is baked into the system at every level. There is a moral, economic and political imperative to reduce waste and increase impact.

This chapter will show that there are four drivers of waste:

- *Piecemeal initiatives*
- *Focus on symptoms, not causes*
- *Inability to scale, replicate and sustain impact*
- *Corruption.*

Although corruption garners most of the headlines, it is the epidemic of piecemeal initiatives which drives most waste. If waste is to be reduced, a new approach is needed by NGOs, funders and governments. This chapter shows how each stakeholder can change their approach to address the pressing challenges of today.

THE CHALLENGE OF WASTE

It is not revealing any secrets to say that much aid money and effort is wasted. At the macro level, the challenge of waste has three standout problems:

- Aid dependency, which inhibits growth through development
- Corruption leakage, and aid may reinforce corrupt habits
- Failure to develop: aid may prop up corrupt regimes and prevent development.

We can leave that debate to the Davos crowd, although a couple of statistics may make them chew on their canapés a little longer:

- Africa receives roughly $50 billion of aid annually.
- Illicit financial flows out of Africa are roughly $50 billion annually,* although these are hard to estimate and do not capture the full scale of local corruption.
- Aid represents nearly half of some African (and Pacific Island) governments' revenues. In a few cases, aid *exceeds* government revenues.[†]

These data points do not fully capture the scale of waste. At the macro level, it is not clear whether aid has helped development. China has lifted a billion people out of poverty without aid; across Africa, however, aid has not had a similar effect. The arguments about aid should not blind us for the urgent need for humanitarian relief in the face of disaster, nor should they be an excuse for not helping the poorest who survive on the edge. Instead, they should focus our minds on how to put the generosity of donors to best effect.

The view from the top of the mountain in Switzerland is very different from the view at the bottom of the mountain in Africa or elsewhere. At the top of the mountain, you see the big picture: policies and the flow of billions of dollars into different priorities. At the bottom of the mountain, you see the poverty and you see extraordinary people making extraordinary efforts to make things better. The

---

*United Nations Economic Commission for Africa: https://www.uneca.org/sites/default/files/PublicationFiles/agr4_eng_fin_web_11april.pdf
†World Bank: https://data.worldbank.org/indicator/DT.ODA.ODAT.XP.ZS

tragedy is that these efforts are often wasted, for all the reasons that this book has outlined:

- Piecemeal initiatives, making it hard to effect change at a system level.
- Focus on symptoms not causes, driven by short-term focus and the need to show 'results'.
- Inability to scale, replicate and sustain impact.
- Corruption.

This chapter explores each of these drivers of waste and suggests a better way forward.

THE DRIVERS OF WASTE
Piecemeal initiatives

In a highly fragmented system, piecemeal initiatives are more or less inevitable. The US Department of State estimates that there are 1.5 million NGOs working in the United States alone.* Many of them sustain heroic efforts to improve the world. But fragmentation does not solve the problems of hunger, poor health housing and education, or climate change. These are deep problems which need deep solutions. Reducing poverty or improving education requires change at a system level.

Both NGOs and funders are incentivized to chase small, piecemeal initiatives where they can show that they have made a difference. Grants officers in foundations need to show that their grants have achieved something. NGOs need to prove to the grants officers that they have delivered as required by the grants officer.

The fragmentation of effort is reinforced by the nature of NGOs and charities, which all assume a remarkable life force of their own. The unstated mission of every charity is to stay in business. The staff do not want to lose their jobs and the board do not want to lose their status and dinner party conversation. This is why there are so few charity mergers and so few wind themselves up voluntarily.

---

*https://www.state.gov/non-governmental-organizations-ngos-in-the-united-states/

In any organization self-interest and self-preservation come first. This means that every NGO and every foundation pushes its own agenda hard. They want to 'prove' that they are making a difference on their own terms, but random acts of kindness are not an effective way of dealing with systemic problems.

BUILDING CASTLES OUT OF SAND

Piecemeal approaches may not only be wasteful, they can even be harmful. For instance, Blackpool (a struggling seaside town in Northern England) wanted to improve the quality of education in its schools. This is a relatively contained problem in theory, but in practice, it requires a range of actors to work together:

- Social services to support parents and children
- Employer engagement to support employability training and skills
- Specialists in literacy, numeracy and behaviour management
- Support for children with special educational needs
- Co-ordination between the local PRU (Pupil Referral Unit) and schools to manage pupils at risk of exclusion from school
- Police to tackle knife crime and drug dealing, which is a cause and symptom of poor education
- Local council to tackle housing so that children have a safe home to return to after school.

During one visit, a local head teacher complained: 'Please just stop all these initiatives. We have too many initiatives, we cannot manage them all. We need to focus on teaching, not on non-stop initiatives.' Fragmented initiatives had become the problem, not the solution.

If you want to build castles, you need the right foundations, a wide variety of skills and deep resources. Otherwise, you can stick to building sandcastles on Blackpool beach: entertaining, but not effective.

Focus on symptoms, not causes

Focus on symptoms, not causes is a direct result of fragmentation in the system.

The aid space is highly competitive. Each NGO and each funder needs to prove that they are having an impact and they need to show it fast if they are to continue funding. As an NGO you can never prove that you have changed the system as a whole: that takes too long, the scope is too broad and it is impossible to prove causality between your intervention and the improvement in the system. There are simply too many other variables which might affect the performance of the system as a whole.

As a result, NGOs and funders often focus on what is easy, not what is important. Endless initiatives are ploughed into aid-friendly countries like Kenya and Uganda. Finding NGOs who are ready to work in fragile states and hostile environments like Somalia or Northern Mali is much harder. They also focus on what is easy to prove. It is easy to prove that you have distributed textbooks. It is also easy to prove that a cohort of girls in a few schools have improved their literacy. These are the sort of things that keep funders happy: they can show pictures of the textbooks and of smiling girls. However worthy such initiatives may be, they give no clue as to how the education system as a whole can be improved at scale and sustainably.

Inability to scale, replicate and sustain impact

Scale should be the friend of NGOs and charities. If you want to change the world, you need world scale. But scale is more often the enemy, not the friend of NGOs. Everything is in favour of keeping things small for an NGO:

- It is easier to raise $1 million a year than to raise $1 billion a year.
- It is easier to prove results if you are working on a discrete problem than a large, complex problem with many variables.
- It is easier to generate results on a small programme, where you can overinvest financially and personally.

215

- Founders find it easier to stay in personal control of one small programme than many huge programmes.

Where NGOs do scale, it is often for the wrong reasons: they want to plant their flag around the world; they want to become major business partners to governments and aid agencies; they want careers for their staff and status for their board. Only lip service to the mission remains. The main goal of the NGO becomes the goal of staying in business.

Corruption

The bird's-eye view of corruption tends to focus on the autocrats and kleptocrats of poor countries who amass fortunes which are stashed away in Swiss Bank accounts. That high-level corruption is clearly very damaging, but there is also endemic low-level corruption embedded in the system. In many countries, corruption is how low-level officials make ends meet, or help them achieve the lifestyle to which they aspire.

In practice, charities are hard-pressed to resist low-level corruption. If you want to operate in an area, it is hard to play to different rules. At the most basic level, failure to pay an attendance fee means you do not meet any officials, unless you are prepared to spend many days sitting in a corridor outside their office being ignored. And in practice, the line between acceptable behaviour and corruption is not as clean as we would like it to be (see the box below).

AT WHAT POINT DOES CORRUPTION START?

It is easy to take a moral stand against corruption. What is easy in theory is hard in practice, not least because corruption can be very insidious. It starts with following local custom and practice, and ends with a call from the District Attorney. So where does corruption start?

- Offering refreshments at a meeting, all the way through to hosting a big feast at a fancy resort.
- Paying for the travel expenses of civil servants attending a meeting, from a local bus fare to first-class international flights.
- Paying the customary attendance fees for civil servants, from a couple of dollars to $200 dollars or more.
- Offering informal personal and professional advice to helping family members secure a place at a prestigious school or university.
- Inviting a government minister to a local conference through to inviting them to a global conference, all expenses paid.
- Paying off a policeman for a fictional traffic offence and paying a 'facilitation' fee to get the doctor to see you fast.

NGO policies should help draw a line between what is acceptable and unacceptable. These lines can quickly become blurred because there is an arms race between NGOs to curry favour with decision makers. When the stakes are highest, the moral dilemma becomes hardest: do you pay off the officials to get aid to the starving refugees, or do you let them die?

If charities succumb to the pressure to follow local custom and practice, they embed the system of corruption. Given that the NGO space is fragmented and competitive, NGOs need to show results. They cannot show results if they have spent months waiting for meetings with officials who hold the key to giving them approval for their activities locally. When charities succumb to corruption they help solve one problem (through the initiative they implement) but they entrench the bigger problem of corruption and waste.

REDUCING WASTE AND INCREASING IMPACT: LESSONS FOR STAKEHOLDERS

The solution starts with funders: philanthropists, aid agencies and donor governments. NGOs can only do what funders let them do.

The current system is highly dysfunctional. All the players need to change.

Governments
Government ministers are often driven to distraction by charities and NGOs. Many NGOs claim to have solved a thorny issue and also claim to have the results to show it. They create huge moral pressure to fix the issue and demand government funding. A solution which is obvious to the charity is rarely so obvious to government, for four reasons:

- Each charity only offers part of a very complex solution.
- Most charities are sub-scale and lack the capacity and capability to deliver at large scale.
- Governments cannot manage policy by integrating the work of 80,000 charities.
- The results the charity claim to achieve are rarely scalable, replicable and sustainable. Even if the results are valid, they rely too much on the dedication of a few individuals.

Inevitably, government prefers to deliver policy through large partners who have both capacity and scale. Unfortunately, large partners are often better at winning bids than delivering results: they know how to maximize their income and minimize their risk by transferring the risk back to government or on to their suppliers.

But charities can fill a vital policy vacuum by developing and testing ideas which are far too risky for a government to try. This has the potential to turn policy on its head. Traditionally, policy is made by ministers who are in post for a couple of years and their advisors, who are in post for even less time. Education in the UK has had 20 Secretaries of State and 98 junior ministers in the last 40 years, which is normal. This means policy is made top down by ambitious amateurs who do not have to live with the results of their decisions. They need headlines, not results: the 20 Secretaries of State have announced an average of 88 Statutory Instruments every year for 40 years.* The result is that most policy is better at delivering positive media headlines than delivering long-term change. It certainly delivers confusion to the system. It is also an immoral way to develop policy: essentially, each new policy announcement is an untested experiment on an entire generation of schoolchildren.

By showing what works in practice, charities give policy makers fresh insights and the capability to improve the system sustainably and at low risk by only taking on proven ideas. To achieve this, governments need to:

- Identify good ideas, even if they are unproven. Instead of waiting for charities to come to them, which means charities who lobby best do the best, government needs to search actively and systematically for ideas. Government has to become proactive, not reactive, in dealing with charities and NGOs.
- Measure what works practically. At the moment, no one really knows what is working and what is not. This is not about doing academic, long-term randomized control trials. It's about taking a business approach to innovation: see what works at a small scale, then do sequentially bigger tests at speed until you reach scale.
- Help charities scale. This means actively investing in capacity building, incubating successes and encouraging mergers. Charities cannot scale themselves, they need structured and focused help. This requires an explicit policy and self-funding budget for government to manage charities, which can help develop and deliver government policy.

This means governments need to take a much more activist approach to realizing the potential which is sitting in their backyard. It almost

---

*Wall, Warriner and Luck. The Need for Policy Stability in Education, December 2019 working paper v2.2.

certainly also requires new institutions or vehicles which can help government identify the best ideas, measure them and scale them. It is a small investment which could yield large gains long term; it could even generate positive media headlines in the short term.

Philanthropists and donors

Philanthropists naturally want to show what they have got for the money they have invested. Having a building named after you is an easy way to show a return on investment. It is also relatively easy to measure outputs such as the number of wells dug, the number of vaccinations given or the number of textbooks donated. Measuring outcomes, not outputs, is harder.

Inevitably, the temptation is to measure what is easy to measure, not what is important to measure. The really important things which change the world, such as eliminating poverty, improving education, reducing crime, addressing climate change and pollution requires complex systemic change. Establishing a causal link between a $1 million donation and an improvement in climate change is close to impossible.

In practice, donors can work with charities in one of three ways:

- *Classic contractor.* This is where the donor essentially buys some results, normally as a result of a persuasive pitch from the charity. There is an inevitable tussle between the donor and the charity over exactly what results should be delivered: the donor will want to push their broad agenda, and the charity will want to push theirs. There is then a search for the segment of the Venn diagram where the interests of both parties overlap. This is the traditional sort of donor–charity relationship and it has limited effectiveness.
- *Investor builder: trust-based philanthropy.* This is where the donor does not invest in specific outcomes, but invests in the charity as a whole, allowing it to build capacity and unrestricted reserves, which are like gold dust. At first, this seems idiotic: why not insist on specific results? If the donor

has a clear focus and a clear theory of change, it should identify those charities which are best aligned with the goals of the donor. If the donor really believes in what the charity is doing, it should invest in building it up instead of investing in short-term results which do not let the charity build capacity. As a contractor, you will have an arms-length relationship with the charity. As an investor builder, you will want to be more of a trusted partner who helps the charity learn, improve its programme, build capacity and scale impact.

- *Strategic investor.* While many donors have a clear view of what they want to achieve, few have a clear view of how they want to achieve it. If you have a clear theory of change, then you should be able to identify the charities which can collectively make the change happen. Like the investor builder, you will help them build capacity, but you will go one step further: you will help build the partnerships or make the mergers which will ensure that collectively, they can deliver the change you want.

Being a classic contractor is relatively easy and reactive. Being a strategic investor is both hard and very proactive. Most donors prefer the comfort zone of being the classic contractor. A few, such as The Peter Cundill Foundation,* are stepping up to new ways of investing. Inevitably, they will make mistakes but in doing so, they will learn how to change the world at a system level.

NGOs and charities
Random acts of kindness are never enough, they can do more harm than good. John (Lord) Bird was a homeless beggar before he founded the *Big Issue*, which helps the homeless. He is clear that giving money

---

*https://www.thepetercundillfoundation.com/ This is one of the earliest foundations to embrace unrestricted funding and moving closer to trust-based philanthropy.

to beggars is cruel, not kind: it cements their feet to the street. They do not need money directly, they need structured help, which is harder and more expensive to deliver in the short term. In the long term, structured help is more likely to help the homeless get off the streets than simply giving money to the person who asks for it. It is not enough to have a heart; you have to use your head as well as your heart to change the world.

The best way you can change the world is by turning your idea into reality, just as Bird took his idea of the *Big Issue* into reality. Charities and NGOs have a vital role to play in bringing new ideas to the table. You can try things which are just too risky for governments and large agencies to try. If you find an idea which works at scale, you can change the world.

- Be ambitious in your goals. If you want to change the world, be clear about how you will do it. Your theory of change will force you to think about the whole system and how you can play a part in helping it change sustainably.
- Be humble about your knowledge. However good your initial idea may be, it will have to change in the face of reality. You can never know all the answers. Be ready to learn from partners, funders and team members. Keep on adapting and improving your idea until it can have replicable, scalable and sustainable impact. Find partners and funders who understand this learning journey of trial and error.
- Be humble about your capacity and capability. Your organization cannot do it all. It will only ever hold one or two parts of the jigsaw. Focus on doing a few things exceptionally well and then work with partners to achieve scale and to deliver the scope of capabilities to deliver change. Focus on scaling the mission, not scaling the organization. Let others take credit.
- Be disciplined. Building an NGO is far harder than building a for-profit organization. In the absence of a profit motive, it is harder to allocate resources; it is harder to generate resources;

you will always be very lean, which means you manage without a financial safety net for mistakes; you cannot borrow to invest and grow. Build the best team you can and build the machine which can deliver for you reliably.

Finally, never lose your enthusiasm for your mission. Winston Churchill is reputed to have said, 'Success consists in staggering from failure to failure without loss of enthusiasm.'* Changing the world is a roller coaster where the lows of failure are very low indeed and the highs of success are exceptionally high. It is the journey of a lifetime which few dare to take. Take it, and you will never look back. But whatever your journey is, enjoy it.

---

*This saying is all over the internet, but repetition does not make the quotation more reliable. Nowhere is there a reliable source which shows where or when Churchill said this.

INDEX